Zion Assembly Church of God

Minutes of the
18th Annual General Assembly

August 31-September 5, 2021

International Ministries Complex
5512 Waterlevel Hwy
Cleveland, Tennessee 37323

Published July 2022

Contents

Historical Assembly Sites..2-3
Explanation of The General Assembly..4-5
Assembly Program, Administration...6-7
Greetings by Superintendent of Operations..8
Welcome by Presiding Bishop...9
Views of the Expansion of the International Ministries Complex...............10
Pre-Assembly Programs...11
Assembly Program...12-28
Assembly Program Adjustments and Attendance...................................29-30
International Staff Reports...31-54
Assembly Business Committee Reports 2021...55-58
Presiding Bishop's Annual Address 2021..59-126
        Introduction..59
        Section I: Fishing With Jesus...62
        Section II: 7x70: The Spirit of Forgiveness..................................73
        Section III: Importance of Doctrine..82
        Section IV: Simple Wedding Band...90
        Section V: Financing the Expansion and Development
                of our International Ministries Complex...............................98
        Section VI: Suffering: A Mark of the Church...............................103
International Appointments 2021-2022..127-128
International Executive Council and International Staff Contact
        Information...129-131
U.S. State Overseers..132
U.S. Overseer's Contact Information..133
U.S. Churches/Missions/Pastors/Church Ministers..............................134-135
U.S. Pastor's Contact Information..136-139
National Overseers...140-141
National Overseers Contact Information...142-144
International Churches/Missions...145-146
Licensed Ministers..147-153
    Bishops..147
    Deacons...147
    Male Evangelists...148
    Female Evangelists..152
    Exhorters...153
Abstract of Faith...154-182
Signature Page: Approval and Verification of Minutes.................................183

Zion Assembly Church of God
International Ministries Center

United Christian Church
(Assembly site 2018)

Historical Assembly Sites

First Assembly House
Murphy, NC

1906

1907

1908-1915

1919-1922

1919-1922

1923-1970

1972-1993

The General Assembly:

The Highest Tribunal of Authority in the Church

The first General Assembly recorded in Acts 15 was a demonstration of the New Testament church's government and divine order. No doubt the unity of the church would have been shattered in its infancy if the decisions of this government had not been respected and obeyed. For the church had become passionately divided in opinion over two issues: namely, the practice of circumcision and certain dietary laws that had been observed under the Old Covenant. The fundamental issue at stake was this: What was the basis of the church's fellowship? Could believing Jews fellowship with believing Gentiles who had not been circumcised and were eating things unlawful under the Old Covenant? These issues were settled in divine order in the council in Jerusalem (A.D. 51/52). This is why our forefathers declared early in our historical development that the **"General Assembly is the highest tribunal of authority in the church on earth."**

Three things are worth noting in examining the procedures and principles followed by the apostles and elders in that first General Assembly:

1. The whole church came together to address the issues, not just the bishops and elders. This is clear from Acts 15.4, 12, 22, 28. The church from the beginning was therefore obviously not an Episcopal or Presbyterian form of government. Moreover, since delegates from many of the local churches were present and participated, and the decisions were kept uniformly by all the churches (vv. 23, 30, 31; 16.4-5), the government was obviously not Congregational in form and practice. It is clear also that, though the apostles and elders led the way in the discussions (15.6-18), everyone present participated and agreed together in the final decisions (vv. 22, 25, 28).

2. The highest authority in this council was God and His Word in Holy Scripture. This may be seen in James' decision [the Council's moderator], which he based on "the words of the prophets" (vv. 15-17), and on what *"seemed good to the Holy Ghost and to us"* (v. 28). This formula—God and His Word in Holy Scripture, the guidance of the Holy Spirit, and the mutual agreement among the Assembly delegates on the meaning of the Scriptures—is what we call "theocratic government." We believe this is the biblical model for church government in distinction from Episcopal, Presbyterian and Congregational models.

4

3. There was a duly recognized order for the meeting and due respect given to its authorized officers in charge: and, not insignificantly, there was also a deep spirituality that had been cultivated and continued among the delegates. One by one those who had something to contribute to the council's understanding were given liberty to speak—Peter, Paul, James (the Lord's brother), et al.—and this brought about the necessary light and understanding to resolve the issues. The believing Pharisees who had been contrary in opinion apparently were enlightened and came into agreement with the final decision. It is possible that some may have went out from this meeting and later joined with the Judaizers to form a dissenting sect (v. 24); but this dissenting sect was certainly not God's church: for it taught and practiced things contrary to the apostles' and elders' doctrine and the church's rule of faith and practice (cf. Acts 15.25-31; 16.4-5).

Too much emphasis cannot be put upon the need for right living and a moderate spirit in the process of discussing and settling issues. Hear the apostle, *"Let your moderation be known unto all men. The Lord is at hand"* (Phil. 4.5). This is of paramount importance. The General Assembly is no place for arrogant, stubborn spirits and self-willed dispositions. On the contrary, love, meekness, and mutual respect among brethren must prevail if the church is going to function in divine order. Further, we are called to "reason together" with God (Is.1.18); after all, all men are finite and prone to misjudgment, only God is infinite and infallible. Therefore, we will *"come to the knowledge of the truth"* only in humbleness of mind and by submitting to the preeminence of the Holy Spirit and the will of God recorded in Scripture.

This special gathering—the General Assembly—should be grounded therefore in much prayer with fasting. Consecrating ourselves through spiritual disciplines is necessary if we want the atmosphere of this important meeting to be charged with the presence of the Lord; and if we truly desire the Holy Ghost to reveal the mind and power of Christ. Only in this way can we answer the apostolic call in Zion Assembly to be *"an holy nation"*—*"an habitation of God through the Spirit,"* and *"the pillar and ground of the truth."*

—WHP

18th Annual General Assembly

Zion Assembly Church of God

August 31-September 5, 2021
International Ministries Complex
5512 Waterlevel Hwy
Cleveland, Tennessee

Program Outline

THEME
"Fishers of Men"

Administration

Presiding Bishop.. Wade H. Phillips

Superintendent of Operations.......................... Anton Burnette

Chief Clerk..Wanda Busbee
    Julia Massey, Sandra Moore, Brenda Reitler, Rita Goodrum, Sandy Morris, Molly Hayward.

Chief Usher..Tod Deakle
    Chad Spicer, Vernon Johnson, J. L. Green, Joey Steele, Daren Childers, Henry Rodriquez, Jerry Nichols, John Bolin.

Chief Registrar...Mandy Thompson
    Shelby Erwin, America Burnette, Victoria Burnette, Marie Carroll, Ally Thompson, Ashley Miller, Rachel McDonald, Emma Erwin.

Assembly Business Committee

Chairman ....Zachary Snyder
                                                        J.J. Davis
             Ricky Graves
             Byron Harris
             Jim C. Orange
             Kevin Clary
             Tod Deakle

Video and Internet Streaming.......................America Burnette
             Jacob Wagner
             Madison Kachel
             Donnie Burnette

Sound Equipment..Jonathan Burnette
             Allen Thompson

Photography..Julie Steele

Projection Director...Tanner Herring

Stage Manager.. Joseph A. Steele

Music.. Kim Erwin, Zachary Snyder

Special Programs Director...............................Wanda K. Busbee

Maintenance/Props..Jim C. Orange

Greetings!

Anton Burnette
Superintendent of Operations

2021 is going to be remembered as a powerful time of the church setting her priorities in order. We turn our eyes to the harvest. With God's help, we are laying the groundwork for fulfilling the Great Commission. The General Assembly this year is a launching pad for the church to fulfill her prophetic destiny and reach the nations with the gospel. Praise God for the General Assembly! We should enter this meeting prayerfully and reverently.

We are glad to be having the Assembly at the International Ministries Complex. We know everyone seemed to love having the Assembly at headquarters last year, so we made improvements to make it possible to hold it here again this year. I hope you enjoy the upgrades and updates we have made to the complex. The following instructions are offered to help ensure that everything will operate and proceed smoothly during each part of the Assembly.

1) Delegates should consult with the appointed Assembly staff (Superintendent of Operations, ushers, stage managers, etc.) in dealing with any problems that may arise during the week.

2) Always remain in designated areas of the building.

3) Food and drink are not allowed in the auditorium, except at the moderator's table (exception is water).

4) If you are on the program and need assistance with equipment, see Anton Burnette.

5) If you need to put pictures, scriptures, etc. on the projection screens, see Anton Burnette.

6) Give soundtracks and media devices to the Sound Engineer before the session in which you are on the program.

7) Observe all parking signs in the church parking lot and also throughout Cleveland.

8) Nursery facilities are provided for your convenience. Observe directional signs.

9) Children's church worship times are posted in the Assembly program.

10) Please refrain from chewing gum in the sanctuary.

We pray and trust that you will enjoy your time in Cleveland and be abundantly blessed in this great 18th General Assembly.

Welcome Delegates!

Wade H. Phillips
Presiding Bishiop

The church is never truer to its essential calling and purpose than when the members from around the world meet to do business for God: to reason together with Him and set forth *"decrees for to keep"* (Acts 15.1-16.5. This is essentially the meaning of the Greek word, *ekklesia*, which is translated "church" in our English versions of the Bible (Mt. 16.17-19; 18.20). It signifies being called out of the kingdom of God, that is, as individuals, and to be joined together by sacred covenant   in the name of Christ to act for Him—to do *"[His] will in earth even as it is in heaven"* (Mt. 6.10; 18.18-19; Mk 13.34; Lk 19.13). The purpose of the General Assembly includes the sacred task of interpreting the Holy Scriptures and acting under a duly appointed order to lay down rules and guidlines for the church around the world: so that we all may *"walk by the same rule," "speak the same thing,"* and be *"perfectly joined together in the same mind and in the same judgement"* (Rom. 15.4-7; 1 Cor. 1.10; Phil. 3.16). What an awesome responsibility!

The General Assembly provides a forum for us to hear from God: proclaim His Word; rekindle the fires of holiness and Pentacostal power; fan the flames of evangelism; stir our affections and deepen our union togerher as on ebody in Christ.

In keeping with the spirit of this Assembly and the theme *"Fishers of Men,"* let us pray and worship together with heartfelt sincerity; and sing and praise together under His authority and in His power and glory!

About the Theme

The Assembly theme *"Fishers of Men"* is meant to stir us up by way of remembrance: that is, to remind us that our primary mission is outreach, eveangelism, and soul winning (Mt. 22.2-10; 28.19-20; Lk 14.17, 21-23). Perfecting [equipping] the saints for the work of the ministry is important (Eph. 4.11-16). but we must first win souls to have people to equip and perfect. Jesus' use of the fishing metaphor is gripping. We are sent to *"catch men"* (Lk. 5.10). Our aim therefore is to learn how to catch men and to ignite a fire within us to go back to our fields of labor and get the work done!

9

Interior view of the newly remodeled auditorium. Exterior and Interior views of the new two-story 10,000 sq. ft. expansion of the International Ministries Complex.

The new expansion wing provides offices for the International Staff and additional space for headquarters operations. It will also facilitate *Zion Assembly Bible College and Seminary* and provide additional space for the School of Ministry Institute. The newly remodeled auditorium in the old building will seat over 350. Adjacent to the auditorium is the new bookstore and gift shop. Also, one of the offices in the original building has been remodeled to provide a nursery.

Pre-Assembly Programs

Minister's Meeting
Tuesday, August 31, 2021

The Annual Ministers' Conference will convene at 10:00 a.m. in the Auditorium of the International Ministries Complex in Cleveland. The meeting is open to all; ministers are especially encouraged to attend and participate. The purpose of the meeting is to promote unity and understanding through prayer and discussion. The preliminary reports by the Assembly Business Committee (ABC) and Doctrine Committee (DC) will be read, and the opportunity will be given to discuss any issues that might need explanation or clarification.

Ministers and Companions Luncheon
(Immediately following the Minister's Meeting) 12:15 p.m.

All ministers and their companions are honored guests at the Ministers' Luncheon. This is sponsored by the International Offices. The luncheon will be held in the Fellowship Hall in the new Educational wing of the International Ministries Complex. **Special singing: Rodriguez Family, CA. Guest speaker: Elijah Wafula, overseer of North Kenya/South Sudan.** Comments and presentations by Dale L. Phillips. Dress code: most of the men prefer to wear suit and tie for this occasion.

Assembly Business and Doctrine Committees
Wednesday, September 1, 2021

The Assembly Business Committee (ABC) will meet again this year at the International Ministries Complex beginning at 9:00 a.m. on Wednesday to finalize its report to present to the 18th Annual General Assembly. The Doctrine Committee (DC) will meet at the same time in a separate room to finalize its report. Anyone who has relevant questions or presentations may interact with the ABC and DC at this time. Personal interviews with the Committees should be arranged through the chairmen.

Assembly Program

Tuesday Evening

6:00 p.m. Worship—**directed by Trevor Graves, KY**

Welcome—**Cleveland Church Young People**
                    —led by Mr. & Mrs. Jacob Wagner

Official Opening of the Assembly

Multi-lingual Concert of Prayer—**Elijah Wafula, Kenya;**
Jorge Estroz, Argentina; David Gomba, Tanzania; Danny Ramirez,
Mexico; J.J. Davis, USA; Nevil Creary, Canada

International Leaders' Personal Reports:

Presiding Bishop

General Executive Council

General Treasurer's Report

Greetings & Special Songs—**California "delegation"**
                    led by Henry Rodriquez

Ladies Ministries Boost—**Pam Jones, director**

Assembly Expense Offering

Presiding Bishop's Annual Address
Section I

Special Songs—**Babs Sullivan, SC**

Message and Invitation—*"The Midnight Cry!"*
                    (Mt. 25.6)—**Bruce Sullivan**

Note: 1) *Kidz' Konvention schedule: Wednesday 6:30-8:00 p.m.; Thursday 1:30-3:30, 6:15-8:00; Friday: 9:30-11:15 a.m.; 6:30-8:00 p.m. Saturday: 8:45-10:00 a.m. 2:30—3:45; 7:00-8:00 p.m. A special Children's program is scheduled for Sunday morning in the Main Auditorium.* **2)** *Attending overseers, turn in your written reports to the Assembly Clerk's table.*

Wednesday Evening

6:30 p.m. Praise and Worship—**Crossville church**

Special Song—**Molly Hayward, MD; Becky Land, SC**

VOZ/ SYNC Boost—L.W. Carter

Media Ministries Report—Anton Burnette

Assembly Expense Offering

Presiding Bishop's Annual Address
Section II

Exhortation by a Mother of "Israel"—**Mary Orange, TN**

Senior Ambassador's Boost—Ruth Tingler, director

"Now also when I am old and gray-headed, O God, forsake me not; until I have shewed thy strength unto this generation, and thy power to every one that is to come" (Ps. 71.18)

Special Singing—**Thompson Family, MS**

Message—*"...I will make you fishers of men"*
(Mt. 4.17)—**Scott E. Neill**

13

Thursday

Note: *Kidz' Konvention today 1:30-3:00, 6:15-8:00 p.m.*

9:00 a.m. **Sunday School Boost**

—**Mandy Thompson, director**

**Camp Reports—Kim Erwin,
International Coordinator**

Special Songs—**Vernon Johnson, MD**

Praise Reports—**Daniel Lucero, CA; Ray Dickson, TN**

Message—*"Inexcusable Excuses"*
(Lk. 14.15-20)—**Anton Burnette**

—Lunch Break—

1:30 p.m. *"Let every thing that hath breath praise the Lord"*
—**Cliff and Becky Kelton, MS**

Special Songs—**TBA**

In Memory . . .

Members: Melvin Morrell, Grace Kelly, Nancy Rebecca Granger, SC; Betty Holstein, TN; Henry Thomas Wright, Jr., AL; Barbara Mayes, VA; Ontoniel Teller, Liliana Sosa De Recinos, Onelia Castellon, German Mazariegos, Guatemala;

Friends: Hulan Ford, Jerry Doan, SC; *Unnamed victims of Covid-19 connected with our churches around the world.*

Message—*" Do the work of an Evangelist"*
(2 Tim. 4.5)—**Daren Childers, KY**

ORDINATION SERVICE

[**Note:** *Ministers and their companions should be seated near the rostrum in preparation for the ordination service*]

—Supper Break—

Thursday Evening

6:15 p.m. Praise and Worship—**Greenville church**

School of Ministry Institute Program
—**Bruce Sullivan, Superintendent**

Assembly Expense Offering

Presiding Bishop's Annual Address
Section III

Special Song—**Becky Land, SC**
Testimonies of God's healing grace—**TBA**
Special Song—**Ashley Davis, WV**

Message—["Made whole by His wounds"]

(Is. 53.4-5)—**Pam Jones**

Healing Line and Prayer

Friday Morning

Attention: The annual SYNC luncheon will be held today at 12:00 in the Fellowship Hall at the International Ministries Complex. L.W. Carter in charge. All SYNC members and invited guests are encouraged to attend.

9:30 a.m.   Praise Him! —**Alex and Holly Drake, KY**

Presiding Bishop's Annual Address
Section IV

Special Songs—**Victoria Green, TN**

Message—*"The Lost Coin"* (Lk. 15.8-10)
                    —**Ricky Graves, KY**

—Afternoon Break—

Friday Evening

[Attention: Front three rows are reserved for Youth Program. All youth [12-35] meet at 8:00 in the Corridor for Youth March]

6:30 p.m.   Special Songs—**West Mobile church**

Message—*"[Making ourselves] all things to all men"*
    (1 Cor. 9.19-22; 10.33; Rom. 15.2-3)—**Pete Sarry, CA**

Shepherding Ministries Boost
                    —**Wilma Carter, director**

Youth Program—**Allen Thompson, director**

*[Attention: **Kidz Konvention today:** 8:45-10:00 a.m.; 2:30-3:45 p.m.; 7:00-8:30 p.m.]*

Saturday Morning

8:45 a.m. Morning Prayer Service—**Eddie and Faye Davis, SC**

9:15   Praise Him!—**Trevor Graves in Concert**

Message—*". . . thou shalt catch men"*
            (Lk. 5.10)—**Tom Brown, WV**

Recognition of Special Guests

—Assembly Choir—
directed by Kari Snyder

Presiding Bishop's Annual Address
Sections V-VI

—Lunch Break—

Saturday Afternoon

2:30 p.m. Worship Him!—**Alicia Harris, MS**

Praise Him!—**Fernando Fermin, CA; Charles Barker, IN**

Praise Reports—**Todd Erwin, KY; Jose Lozano, CA**

Assembly Business Committee Report
Doctrine Committee Report
—Supper Break—

Saturday Evening

7:00 p.m. *"Sing aloud unto God"*
                    —Caledonia church

Words of Wisdom by "Honorable Women"
                    **—Rosie Ramirez, CA; Rose Snyder, WV;
                    Norie Garavito, CA; Jeanette Surratt, SC**

Message—*". . . Go out [quickly] . . . and compel the*
to come in . . ." (Lk. 14.21-23)
                    —Joseph "Buddy" Quillen

Special Singing—**Henry Rodriguez, CA**

Assembly Expense Offering

World Mission Program
Wade H. Phillips, director

—Parade of Nations—

> *"Therefore they shall come and sing
> in the height of Zion . . . and shall flow
> together to the goodness of the LORD . . .*
>   *—Jer. 31.12*

Sunday Morning

9:15 a.m. **Sunday School Lesson—Gavin McDonald, SC**
9:45   Special Singing—**California "delegation"**

Children's Ministries Program
—Kayla Graves, director

—Assembly Choir—

Message—"*. . . all things are ready . . .*"
(Mt. 22.4) —**Todd McDonald, SC**

Announcements

Appointments

Consecration Service

Song: *"Heaven Will Surely Be Worth It All"*
—Debbie, Dreama, and Brenda
led by Zachary Snyder

Heaven will surely be worth it all.
Worth all the sorrows that here befall;
After this life with all its strife,
Heaven will surely be worth it all.

Assembly Appointments
2021-2022

International Executive Council _____

_____

_____

Field Secretary_____

World Mission director_____

Mission Representatives_____

_____

_____

General Treasurer_____

Department of Education/Media Ministries_____

Assistant Publisher_____

Shepherding Ministries director_____

School of Ministry Institute director_____

Fishers of Men director_____

Ladies Ministries director_____

Sunday School director_____

Sunday School Literature Editor_____

Senior Ambassadors director._____

Youth Ministries director_____

Children's Ministries director_____

Camping Coordinator/Advisor_____

Voice of Zion/SYNC Booster_____

Tract Ministries director_____

Executive Secretary_____

Committees

Assembly Business Chairman_____

_____

_____

_____

Doctrine Chairman_____

_____

_____

General Properties Chairman_____

_____

_____

General Trustees_____

_____

_____

National Overseers

Argentina_____

Bangladesh_____

Benin_____

Bolivia_____

Burundi_____

Cambodia_____

Cameroon_____

Canada_____

Chile_____

Costa Rica_____

Democratic Republic of the Congo (DRC)_____

Dominican Republic_____

Ghana_____

Guatemala_____

Guinea_____

Haiti_____

Honduras_____

India Mid-East_____

India South_____

Ivory Coast_____

Kenya North_____

Kenya South_____

Liberia_____

Malawi_____

Mexico North_____

Mexico South_____

Mozambique_____

Myanmar (Burma)_____

Nepal_____

Nicaragua_____

Nigeria_____

Pakistan_____

Paraguay_____

Peru_____

Philippines_____

Rwanda_____

Sierra Leone_____

South Sudan_____

Tanzania_____

Thailand_____

Togo_____

Uganda_____

United States_____

Uruguay_____

Venezuela_____

Zimbabwe_____

Zambia_____

State Overseers

United States:

North Carolina/South Carolina_____

West Virginia/Virginia/Pennsylvania/Maryland_____

Indiana/Kentucky/Michigan/Illinois_____

Tennessee/Georgia_____

Mississippi/Alabama/Louisiana_____

Idaho/Wyoming_____

Colorado/Kansas/Missouri_____

Texas/Arizona/New Mexico_____

California /Nevada_____

Oregon/Washington_____

A Biblical Explanation of the . . . General Assembly

The General Assembly is an extraordinary event because 1) it represents the universal [catholic] expression of the church in worship, fellowship, biblical interpretation, and decision-making; 2) it is essential for the unity and progress of the church; 3) it is the highest tribunal of authority on earth under Christ in matters of faith, practice, discipline, and church government.

In the General Assembly the ministers and members meet together with God in a decision-making capacity: to understand the will of God; to seek His light and guidance for the future course of the church; and to commit themselves to live and work by the resolutions adopted by Assembly. The Assembly represents the one time of the year that we gather together in His name from all over the world to bind and loose in the earth what God has bound and loosed in heaven (Mt. 16.19; Acts 15.1-16.5). We consecrate ourselves to understand the will of God—to find the perfect mind of Christ. This is why in Jacob's words the church is a **dreadful place** (Gen. 28:16, 17); for it is at this special time that the church acts in its official capacity as God's *ekklesia*, having been ordained and authorized by Christ to do so (Mt. 16.9; 18.17; Mk. 13.34; Lu. 19.13; Jn. 20.23; Acts 1.13-21; 6.1-6; 15.1-29). Here in this special meeting, we reason together with God (Is. 1.18; Acts 15.6-19, 28), and the ministers and members look judiciously into the Holy Scriptures (compare Acts 15.15-18 with Amos 9.11, 12) and seek diligently for the Spirit's illumination until an understanding is reached on what is the will of God is (Acts 15.28-29). Then, having come to this understanding, all agree to *"walk by the same rule"* and *"mind the same thing"* (1 Cor.1.10; Phil. 3.16; Acts 16.4-5), that is, we commit ourselves to live and walk together as one body in Christ according to the decisions agreed upon in this sacred meeting.

Because the Bible is the supreme objective authority of the church, the General Assembly is "a judicial body only," that is, all decisions in regard to faith and government that are binding on the ministers and members must be shown to be either explicitly or implicitly in harmony with the teachings of Christ and the apostles.

24

The biblical model for the General Assembly and our judicious process is found in Acts 15.1-29. Here the *apostles and elders* gathered together with the *whole church* (vv. 12, 22, 28), and prayed and deliberated with the help of the Spirit until all were able to "see eye to eye." It is said that the decisions made in the Jerusalem council *"seemed good to the Holy Ghost, and to us"* (v. 28). Then on this basis, all agreed to live by the *"decrees [dogmas] for to keep"* (16.4)—*"And so were the churches established in the faith, and increased in number daily"* (v. 5).

Corporate counsel is thus an underlying principle upon which the government of the church is established. The General Assembly is made up of ministers and members from around the world whom Providence has blessed to participate in the proceedings. The wise man wrote, *"Where no counsel is, the people fall: but in the multitude of counselors there is safety" (Pr. 11.14),* and again, *"Without counsel purposes are disappointed: but in the multitude of counselors they are established"* (15.22).

When Rehoboam was made king in the Old Testament theocracy, it is said that *all Israel* came to Shechem to make him king (1 Kg. 12.1). Moreover, it is emphasized that Rehoboam failed because he did not heed the counsel of the *elders and the people* in making decisions (vv. 6-15); but heeded rather a select counsel of the *young men that were grown up with him* (vv. 8-10), thus signifying that Rehoboam was partial in his decision-making and succumbed to the opinion of the young men who were opposed to the will of God. Indeed, those young men typically were full of themselves: arrogant, boastful, and harsh in their opinions (vv. 10-14).

It will be noticed further, regarding the house of God under Rehoboam, that ultimately the will of God is all that matters, and His will is best discerned and understood by men and women who consecrate themselves to the Lord. In any case, God always ultimately has His way—sometimes in spite of the leaders and the people. *"Wherefore the king hearkened not unto the people; for the cause was from the Lord"* (v. 15; see also v. 24). Tragically, Rehoboam's actions caused the house of God to divide (vv. 16-20), but this division was foreknown in the divine counsel and thus prosecuted according to the will of God. See the prophet Ahijah's prophecy (1 Kg. 11.29-39).

God's fixed purpose in and through David was fulfilled in Christ through the southern kingdom of Judah; nothing could prevent that!

The church under the spirit and terms of the New Covenant operates as *"the habitation of God through the Spirit"* (Eph. 2.22). The ministers and members form the temple of God and are unified through the indwelling power and wisdom of the Spirit. This is the key to theocratic government—the indwelling graces and gifts of the Spirit being allowed to prevail in the church; for the Spirit creates a spiritual dynamic within the church that unites the ministers and members together intrinsically in one body of Christ and illuminates them to understand the will of God. Even before the Spirit was poured out on the day of Pentecost, the 120 were in *one accord* because they had been sanctified and were *"continually in the temple praising and blessing God"* (Lu. 24.53). The essential key to the unity and power of the church is in sanctification, and in maintaining a consecrated devotion to Christ. When everyone's ego is crucified, then Christ rules supreme—the kingdom of God prevails! Thus Christ says in His prayer to the Father, *"Sanctify them through thy truth . . . that they all may be one . . . And the glory which you gave me I have given them . . . that they may be made perfect in one"* (Jn.17.17-23).

It is said following the day of Pentecost that *"the multitude of them who believed were of one heart and of one soul . . . and great grace was upon them all"* (Acts 4.32-33). Likewise, the key to God's glorious government in this last day's Zion depends on our willingness to allow the Spirit to hold sway over us and prevail in matters of faith, practice, government, and the prosecution of the church's mission in the world. The apostle Paul understood this divine principle and encouraged the church to *"walk worthy of the vocation wherewith you are called, with all lowliness and meekness, with longsuffering, forbearing one another in love; endeavoring to keep the unity of the Spirit in the bond of peace"* (Eph. 4.1-3). He went on to say, *"[For] there is one body, and one Spirit, even as you are called in the one hope of your calling; one Lord, one faith, one baptism, one God and Father of all, who is above all, and through you all, and in you all"* (vv. 4-6).

We see then that it is imperative to stir up the graces of Christ within us and labor in prayer to cultivate a heavenly atmosphere in the place where we meet to deliberate and act for God. The power fell on the day of Pentecost because they were together *"In one accord in one place."* And they answered God's call and succeeded because they were of *"one heart and one soul"* and *"great grace was upon them all."*

Should we expect God's blessings to fall on this last day's Zion on the basis of anything less than the basis upon which He blessed that early Zion? Surely not. It is an old principle that cannot be transgressed if we expect the blessings of God to be upon this last day's house: *"Behold, how good and how pleasant it is for brethren to dwell together in unity . . . for there the Lord commanded the blessing"* (Ps. 133.1-3).

We fully expect the prophets' and apostles' vision of the last day's church to be fulfilled in Zion Assembly: *"The glory of this latter house shall be greater than that of the former, says the Lord . . . and in this place I will give peace . . ."* (Hag. 2.9) . . . *"That he might present it to himself a glorious church, not having spot, or wrinkle, or any such thing."* (Eph. 5.27).

—WHP

"And they wrote letters by them after this manner; The apostles and elders and brethren send greeting unto the brethren which are of the Gentiles in Antioch and Syria and Cilicia: Forasmuch as we have heard, that certain which went out from us have troubled you with words, subverting your souls, saying, Ye must be circumcised, and keep the law: to whom we gave no such commandment: It seemed good unto us, being assembled with one accord, to send chosen men unto you with our beloved Barnabas and Paul, Men that have hazarded their lives for the name of our Lord Jesus Christ. We have sent therefore Judas and Silas, who shall also tell you the same things by mouth. For it seemed good to the Holy Ghost, and to us, to lay upon you no greater burden than these necessary things . . . And as they went through the cities, they delivered them the decrees for to keep, that were ordained of the apostles and elders which were at Jerusalem. And so were the churches established in the faith, and increased in number daily."
—Acts 15.23-28; 16.4-5

Assembly Sites
2004 - 2021

Ramada Inn & Convention Center, Pigeon Forge
Site of First Annual Assembly 2004

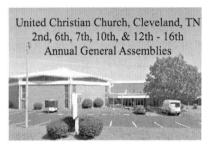

United Christian Church, Cleveland, TN
2nd, 6th, 7th, 10th, & 12th - 16th
Annual General Assemblies

T.L. Lowery Center, Cleveland, TN
8th Annual General Assembly

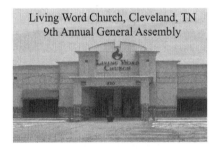

Living Word Church, Cleveland, TN
9th Annual General Assembly

Bridgewater Place, Knoxville, TN
11th Annual General Assembly

Int'l Ministries Complex, Cleveland, TN
3rd-6th, 9th, 17-18th Annual General Assemblies

Assembly Program Adjustments

**The Assembly program proceeded
as scheduled with the following exceptions:**

*Note: The Presiding Bishop read the various sections
of his address throughout the Assembly.*

Administrative Adjustments

Additional clerks who served throughout the Assembly:
Kim Merrill, Sally Carrillo, Charity Plasse, Ally Thompson,
Juanita Pyles, Donna Pounders, Rose Snyder,
Renetta Kelton, Becky Kelton, Marie Llaneza
[Absent: Julia Massey, Sandra Moore, Rita Goodrum, Sandy
Morris, Billie Smith, Molly Hayward, Rosa Nicholson]

Additional Administrative assistance
Music, Spencer Plasse [Kim Erwin, absent]
Usher, Cody Major [Jerry Nichols, absent]
Stage Manager, Charles Barker [Tanner Herring, absent]

Tuesday

Wilma Carter served as guest speaker during
Minister's Luncheon for Elijah Wafula

Jose Lozano prayed during the multi-lingual prayer.
[absent ministers: Elijah Wafula, Danny Ramirez, Nevil Creary]

General Treasurer's Report was given on Saturday afternoon during
the business committee report

Ladies Ministries report was read by Wanda Busbee
in the absense of the director, Pam Jones.
Wanda Busbee also boosted the Ladies Retreat

29

Thursday

Mandy Thompson gave camp report
[Kim Erwin, absent]

Special songs by Molly Hayward and the Snyder family
in place of Vernon Johnson (MD) [absent]

Praise reports were given by David Gomba (TZ) and
Leyre Hernandez (CA) in place of Daniel Lucero (CA)
and Ray Dickson (TN)

In Memory . . .
Correction: Hulan Ford was a member of Zion Assembly

During Presiding Bishop's evening Annual Address, Bishops David
Gomba and Jorge Estroz gave praise reports of healings

Saturday

8:45 am prayer service was led by Jim and Mary Orange
[Eddie and Faye Davis (SC), absent]

Message—". . . thou shalt catch men," preached by J.J. Davis
[Tom Brown (WV), absent]

Words of Wisdom by "Honorable Women"
Priscilla Pompa
[Jeanette Surratt (SC), absent]

2:30 p.m. worship was led by Zach Snyder
[Alicia Harris (MS), absent]

Registered attendance: 446

Presiding Bishop's Report
Eighteenth Annual General Assembly
August 31, 2021–September 5, 2021

Note: This report reflects my work from the last day of the
Assembly last year to last night, September 4, 2021.

"As the hart panteth for the water brooks,
So panteth my soul for Thee, 0 God. My soul
thirsts for God, for the living God" (Ps. 42.1-2).

With a thankful heart I magnify the name of the Lord for His
sustaining grace and strength another year, and for the anointing
poured out upon me to fulfill the duties and responsibilities
connected with this sacred position. Our churches have continued
to labor faithfully this year in spite of the Covid-19 pestilence and
many tribulations; for which I am thankful.

In some ways it has been a trying year. We have been
opposed on many fronts but have emerged victorious in every
case. Even in the most trying moments we behold our glorious
Savior who was elevated by His Father to overcome all the
contradictions of demons and men. Following in the inspired
counsel of the writer of Hebrews, we always in the most trying
times keep "looking unto Jesus, the author and finisher of our faith,
who for the joy that was set before Him endured the cross, despising
the shame, and has sat down at the right hand of the throne of
God" (Heb. 12.2-3). Like our blessed Lord, we too are promised
to be exalted in due time if we remain steadfast in the faith
(Rom. 8.37-39; 1 Pet. 5.6; Jas. 4.10; 1 Jn. 5.4-5; Rev. 3.20-22).

I want to use this occasion to impress upon us something
that is vitally important: namely, the need to "esteem [our leaders]
very highly in love for their work's" sake (1 Thess. 5.12), and
to follow them "who have the rule over [us]" and "imitate their
faith" (Heb. 13.7, 17; see also 1 Cor. 4.16; 11,1; Phil 3.17; 1
Thess. 1.6; et al.). Well, you might say, leaders are just men; but,
see, they are men whom God has called, chosen, ordained, and

appointed to oversee the work of His church (Acts 20.28; Mt. 16.19; 25.45; Mk. 13.34; Jn. 20.23). So, in that sense, they are not ordinary men. Think about the pointed advice of the apostles and prophets as they were moved by the Holy Ghost to give us inspired counsel along these lines. While our leaders are all men, of course; yet they have been called by God and ordained to fulfill the ministry that God has laid upon them. Recall the passage in Ex. 22.28: "Thou shalt not speak evil of the ruler of thy people." Many fail to realize how damaging and counterproductive it is to criticize and belittle the governors and leaders of the church. In my view nothing has damaged and stunted the growth of the church more than the sin of belittling and criticizing its leaders. For, see, when you diminish the image of leadership you hurt and hinder the whole church. It discourages and disillusions the sheep and the "other sheep" looking on.

It is hard to see how one can love the church and at the same time slander its leaders and diminish their influence. To transgress against this counsel recalls the old adage, "you cut off your nose to spite your face." So brethren, heed the apostolic advice: "Be slow to speak" and slower yet to criticize those over you in the Lord, lest, as the wise man says, your criticism becomes a snare for your own soul as well as damaging to the whole church. Remember the saying, "Loose lips sink ships" (Prov.10.19- 21; 17.27-28; 18.2-7, 13; Jas. 1.19).

Now regarding the practical work connected with my office: I serve as the primary presbyter among all the presbyters throughout the world; and consequently have been involved in several disciplinary actions to maintain proper order in the church. This includes examining and ordaining elders, issuing licenses to new ministers, but also, unfortunately, having to discipline and even revoke the credentials of a few misguided and disorderly mm1sters, including one national overseer. I have answered all correspondence and calls that have come into the office—roughly 500 letters and e-mails and 2250 phone calls; kept up a regular correspondence with the national and state overseers and the International Staff; served as the editor in-chief of our church magazine, the Voice of Zion; prepared and taught lessons for SMI; served as World Mission Secretary with the cheerful and able assistance of Anton Burnette, Wanda Busbee, Yomi Adekunle [Nigeria], David Gomba [Tanzania], Miguel Garcia, Jr., Danny Ramirez, Jorge Estroz [Argentina], and Nolvin Hernandez [Honduras].

I want to thank our executive secretary, Wanda Busbee, for her assistance and untiring labors in many areas of the work, including World Missions, preparation and publication of the Voice of Zion, and lending a helpful hand in almost all areas of the work connecting with the responsibilities of the Presiding Bishop, including preparing and presiding over the General Assembly. [She is also the local church clerk and treasurer and active in all the phases of the work in the Cleveland church].

Hundreds of ministers and members were given counsel both in the office and on the field. I have worked with the Executive Council, the Assembly Business Committee, the Doctrine Committee, the overseers, pastors, and ministers to promote the work in all of its various dimensions and operations. I want to thank the International Staff and the national and state overseers who have cheerfully cooperated with me in the promotion of the work. Most of our leaders sacrificed to move the work forward in their regions and throughout the world, and several performed exceptionally well. I want to take this opportunity also to commend the companions of our overseers and international workers; for they have helped to carry the load of the work.

Overseeing the construction of the new building and remodeling of the original facilities consumed a great deal of my time and energy. Again I was greatly assisted by Bishop Burnette, Steve and Glenda Major, Alice Jones, Jim Orange, and several others from the Cleveland church.

In regard to writing, we published the Gospel of the Kingdom of God this year (a 264 page work with notes on the basics of the Kingdom). This book will be required reading for our School of Ministry Institute students. Also the second volume of the Annual Addresses (which includes five addresses, 2016-2021) should be sent to the printers in the next couple of months. With the assistance of Wanda Busbee, Rosa Nicholson, Renetta Kelton, and America Burnette, and others we have begun to update several books I had written while in our former fellowship. These books will be republished through Zion Assembly Church of God Publishing House. At least two of these books—God the Church and Revelation and The Nature of the Church should be completed this Assembly year. Rosa Nicholson is also translating into Spanish, The Mystery of Sin, which is also required reading for SMI students. What about the second volume of We have had two or three hundred inquiries [from outside and inside the church] regarding the second volume of Quest to Restore God's House. It will cover the years 1924-1990. I have begun to write this volume (about 175 pages so far) but, regretfully, we have had to set it aside numerous times to give attention to more urgent matters connected with the office and responsibilities of the Presiding Bishop. All I can say at this point is that I'm working on it. "Let patience," brethren, "have her perfect work!"

I want to thank my faithful wife, Dale, for her support and love for the church. Like the ideal woman in Prov. 31.10-31, ["She willingly works with her hands; girds herself with strength; reaches out to the poor and needy; is hospitable; and her husband safely trusts and praises her"].

Finally, I want to thank each of you for the many prayers you have offered up in behalf of my family, and also for the many kindnesses that you have shown to us. May the Lord richly bless and keep you in the power of His saving grace.

The following are some personal statistics in regard to the work.

Sermons Preached.................................171

Converted..3

Sanctified..2

Holy Ghost Baptisms...............................2

Added to the church................................1

Baptized in Water....................................0

Tithes paid..................................$5,400.00

Offerings given.............................$8,680.00

Miles traveled..................................27,850

Revivals conducted.................................1

Churches visited.....................................7

Regional Conventions Attended.....................3

General Assembly (Moderated)......................1

Thank you again for your prayerful support and cooperation, and for the many kindnesses you have shown to me and my family. May the Lord bless and keep you in His great love and power.

Humbly submitted,

Wade H. Phillips

2012 was the first year that the Presiding Bishop's Commendation Award was bestowed upon deserving members. It has since become an annual Assembly event.

The following have been recipients of this award:

2012
Honoria Garavito, CA
William (Bill) Reid, TN
Joshua Amara, Africa

2013
Marie Spurling Crook, TN
Miguel Garcia, Sr., CA
Dale L. Phillips, TN

2014
Yomi Adekunle, Nigeria
Glenda Major, CA
Danny Ramirez, CA

2015
Robert Barron Ramirez, CA
Wanda K. Busbee, SC
Alice Jones, TN

2016
Jeanette Surratt, SC
Donna Pounders, MS
Saintainel Hostelus, Haiti

2017
Ricky Graves, KY
Gavan McDonald, SC
Zachary Snyder, AL

2018
Charles and Mary Barker, IN
Clifford and Becky Kelton, MS
Robert and Maria Llaneza, NC

2019
Richard and Kim Merrill, OR
Becky Land, SC
Dave and Judy Ashley, WV

2020
Dave & Deanna Sanner, WV
L.W. & Wilma Carter, VA
Jose Manuel Lazano, CA

2021 Recipients
of the Presiding Bishop's Commendation Award:

Rick and Stephanie Ferrell, TN
Ambrosio "Roberto" Lopez, CA
James "Jim" Orange, TN

Department of Education/Media Ministries Report

to the Eighteenth Annual General Assembly
September 1, 2021

"For so hath the Lord commanded us, saying, I have set thee to be a light of the Gentiles, that thou shouldest be for salvation unto the ends of the earth" –Acts 13.47

I am thankful for the opportunity to serve the Lord and His church in regards to the Education and Media departments throughout this Assemby year. I want to thank my wife, Grace, and our children for supporting me in this position, constantly providing me with prayers and assistance where needed. As overseer, I want to thank the state of Tennessee, and as pastor, the Cleveland and Pulaski congregations for supporting me in the broader mission of the church.

I appreciate being able to work daily with our Presiding Bishop. He is a well of wisdom and knowledge that I go to often to assist me in the work for which I am responsible.

The year has had many interesting twists and turns. I left the Assembly last year and immediately faced a battle with Covid-19. I am thankful that my case was comparatively mild, and I quickly recovered. This pandemic has been a constant reminder of the frailty of our lives but also of the power of our God.

I want to again commend our pastors for staying in contact with their members by text, phone, and social media through the Pandemic, and for making their services available by Facebook, Youtube, and Zoom.

We streamed the weekly services of the Cleveland church and also several headquarters events including the General Assembly, Youth Convention, and several classes from the School of Ministry.

Received several reports from around the world from people who have been blessed by these live streams and video archives.

I am thankful for each one who has enjoyed these services online, and for the many letters, messages, texts, and calls of encouragement. Media ministries is making available another avenue for fellowship, encouragement, and outreach.

This year we accumulated 25, 900 views on Youtube and picked up 121 new subscribers, bringing our total to 543 subscribers. Through this system of outreach, we have made several new contacts with individuals, nationally and internationally. All the media work completed is with the desire of building our local churches and establishing new missions.

I take the theme of this Assembly, "Fishers of Men," as a challenge for the media and education departments to go further in assisting to fulfill the great commission.

Below is a concise report of my activities for the year:

1. Consistently worked towards the vision and goals for the education and media departments.
2. Worked with the Presiding Bishop and others in overseeing the expansion of headquarters and the future home of our Bible College and on the renovation of the sanctuary at headquarters.
3. Updated the Zion Assembly web properties as needed.
4. Coordinated with the Missions Department regarding new international contacts, being a point of contact for national overseers, and assisting the Treasurer with all international allotment and funding.
5. Continued to adapt online content creation plan for Zion Assembly. Emphasizing the best way to represent the church online.

6. Ministered and streamed the Cleveland church services live.

7. Attended, instructed, and streamed at the School of Ministry Institute in Tennessee.

8. Attended the Mississippi/Alabama State Convention and conducted the Tennessee State Convention.

9. Attended and worked in two Youth Camps, Camp Jubilee, and Camp Hosanna.

10. Attended and streamed the Youth Convention in Cleveland, TN.

11. Attended Executive Council meetings in Pigeon Forge, TN and Cleveland, TN.

12. Submitted my monthly reports and tithes.

Thanks to my wife, my children and our home church for their constant support and love.

Humbly submitted,
Anton Burnette
Director of Education/Media

General Treasurer's Report
Greetings to the 18th Annual General Assembly

"And whatsoever ye do, do it heartily, as to the Lord, and not unto men; knowing that of the Lord ye shall receive the reward of the inheritance: for ye serve the Lord Christ" –Col. 3.23-24

I am grateful to God for His mighty hand that has been upon me this year and for all opportunities to serve in His glorious church. His blessings are immeasurable, and I owe Him everything.

In February I was appointed to the office of General Treasurer when unforeseen circumstances prevented Pam Jones from completing her appointment. The experience has been both gratifying and humbling. I was honored to witness first hand the selfless, dedicated, and cheerful work ethic of the General Staff, and I was humbled by the magnitude of work accomplished through the ministry and membership of the church this year. I appreciate our Presiding Bishop for his prayerful support and for allowing me the privilege of serving the church under this appointment. I would like to thank Pam Jones for her help and guidance. It made for a smooth and successful transition. A very special thank you to my wonderful husband, Cecil, for his encouragement, patience, and continual prayers during my trips to and from Cleveland. Without his support, I may not have had the privelege to be a part of this great work. He is truly my constant helpmate.

As General Treasurer, I managed the finances of the International Offices. I processed and filed monthly ministerial reports as well as those of the local churches. I disbursed approved quarterly mission allotments, prepared various monthly reports for the Presiding Bishop, and processed monthly payroll. In accordance with my appointment, I have prepared and will present to this General Assembly the 2021 Annual Treasurer's Report. The document contains a summarized account of any and all receipts and expenditures as well as account totals for this fiscal year July 2020 through June 2021 and will be read as part of this report.

Respectfully Submitted
Donna Pounders
General Treasurer

Zion Assembly Church of God
18th. Annual General Assembly
Financial Summary
July 1, 2020 - June 30, 2021

Summary of Accounts

Accounts:	Balance Forward	Income	Account Tranfers-In	Account Tranfers-Out	Expenses	Ending Balance
United Comm Bank(Operating)	234,296.90	393,892.94		311,287.08	316,902.76	0.00
Smart Bank (Operating)	0.00	366,253.06	311,287.08		281,354.91	396,185.26
IPBF Money Market Acct.	220,344.11	328.44		45,500.00		175,172.55
Paypal Account	79.34		25,016.79	24,867.13		229.00

Account: SmartBank	Balance Forward	Deposited	Transfers In	Transfers Out	Expenses	Ending Balance
Smart Bank (ME - Mission Funds)	1,977.78		67,614.09	68,764.44		827.43

Accounts: Misc.	Balance Forward	Received		Transfer to Paypal	Expenses & Fees	Ending Balance
Paypal on Line	0.00	25,805.65		25,016.79	742.81	46.05
Petty Cash	15.18				15.18	0.00
TOTALS:	$456,713.31	$786,280.09	$403,917.96	$475,435.44	$599,015.66	$572,460.29

Fund Balances in Checking Account:

Fund	Balance Forward	Income / Transfer In	Expenses / Transfers Out	Ending Balance
Bible College Operating Fund	-455.49	455.49		0.00
Emergency Fund	13,598.57	4,226.25	312.00	17,512.82
Ladies Retreat Fund	13,219.59	9,130.00	13,289.85	9,059.74
IYC Retreat Fund	2,648.87	0.00	300.00	2,348.87
Missions Fund (Inc. & Exp.)	66,245.64	188,258.57	84,814.73	
(20% Mission trf. out to IPBF Fund)			35,325.87	
(20% Mission trf. out to IPBF MM)			1,930.35	132,085.97
(trf out to Smartbank)				
School of Ministry Institute	14,082.41	11,754.32	5,146.88	20,689.85
IPBF Fund (Income & Expenses)	16,895.48	190,307.46	89,791.33	
(IPBF trf in fro. 20% Mission / out to MM)		35,325.87		
Trf. Out - to Underwrite Loan Paymen			50,398.12	102,339.39
Sunday School Fund	31,250.59	18,453.85	10,825.00	38,879.44
Tithe Fund	71,914.97	247,832.21	297,387.55	
Trf in fr. IPBF to Underwrite Loan Payment		50,398.12		72,757.75
Voice of Zion Fund	2,305.04	8,890.00	3,835.39	7,359.65
Youth-Media Fund	2,581.23	6,116.11	15,546.16	-6,848.22
TOTALS	$234,286.90	$771,148.25	$608,903.23	$396,185.26

Income Statement
Year ending June 30, 2021

Total Contributions:
$786,280.09

Total Expenses:
$599,015.66

NET INCOME:
$187,264.43

ZION ASSEMBLY CHURCH OF GOD

Financial Report *UPDATE FOR ASSEMBLY* for the months of July & August 2021

	Emer.	Ladies Ret	IYC	Missions	SMI	VOZ	SS	Tithe	IPBF	Y-Media	Totals
Bal. Forward	$17,512.82	$9,059.74	$2,348.87	$132,085.97	$20,689.85	$7,359.65	$38,879.44	$72,757.75	$102,339.39	-$6,848.22	$396,185.26
Transfer In								$6,092.20	$790.48		$6,882.68
Income	$1,146.00	$0.00	$0.00	$4,299.66	$748.95	$75.00	$3,182.84	$31,245.48	$7,540.98	$1,134.29	$49,373.20
Payments	$0.00	$0.00	$0.00	$1,800.00	$0.00	$877.40	$0.00	$39,313.44	$25,582.35	$1,309.38	$68,882.57
Transfer Out				$790.48					$6,092.20		$6,882.68
Ending Bal.	$18,658.82	$9,059.74	$2,348.87	$133,795.15	$21,438.80	$6,557.25	$42,062.28	$70,781.99	$78,996.30	-$7,023.31	$376,675.89

TOTAL OF ACCOUNTS

Bal. Checking	$376,675.89
IPBF MM	$175,186.95
Smart Bank - Mission Funds	$176.43
Smart Bank - PayPal Acc.	$140.70
Total Funds	**$552,179.97**

International Executive Council Report

Since the close of the 2020 General Assembly, the Executive Council met twice in Cleveland to work with the Presiding Bishop on matters brought before the Council. The Council also participated in the minister's meeting in Pigeon Forge, and each Council member attended the School of Ministry Institute in Cleveland.

The bishops on the council are as follows:

> Wade H. Phillips
> L.W. Carter
> Scott Neill
> Joseph Steele
> Anton Burnette
> Rick Ferrell (Secretary)

As we are challenged in this Assembly to be fishers of men, let us be reminded of the words of Jesus in John 9.4, *"I must work the works of him that sent me, while it is day; the night cometh, when no man can work."*

This Council was commissioned in 2015 to "interact with the Presiding Bishop in the oversight of the church." We covet your prayers in this regard. We have taken in hand the task of understanding the will of the Lord and to expound on the vision the Lord has given our Presiding Bishop to move Zion Assembly ahead to be effective "Fishers of Men."

Respectfully Submitted,
Rick Ferrell
Secretary

Voice of Zion/SYNC Ministries Report

Greetings to the 18ᵗʰ Annual General Assembly

The Lord gave the word: ***"Great was the company of those that published it."***—Ps. 68.11

This year has been another year filled with various obstacles, but the Lord so graciously brought us through them all.

That old song, *"Amazing Grace,"* states, "Through many dangers, toils, and snares, I have already come; 'tis grace hath brought me safe thus far, and grace will lead me home."

We have had a great year in getting new subscriptions for the *Voice of Zion* magazine. The wonderful members of Zion Assembly use this magazine to spread the good news of the gospel and promote the church.

The Lena King Club has grown also. Thank God for members like her and others who have subscribed 10 new persons. I thank all of you for your participation.

We covet your prayers to help us reach the whole world with this message.

To God be the Glory,
L.W. Carter, *VOZ*/SYNC Ministries Booster

International Sunday School Report

Greetings to the 18th Annual General Assembly

It has been an honor to serve in the capacity of Sunday School Director for another year. As Sunday School Director, I have worked alongside Brother Bruce Sullivan, Sunday school literature editor, and Brother Anton Burnette, director of media ministries, to make sure the Sunday school literature is made available to everyone on the church's website. We offer children, teen, and adult lessons with a large print option for adults in English and Spanish.

I have spent this last year writing new children's Sunday school literature, which includes a teacher's guide and a weekly family reading plan. I have worked alongside Brother Allen Thompson who is writing new teen Sunday school literature. The new teen lessons are designed to engage the students in daily Bible reading leading into each week's lesson. I have also been in communication with Brother Bruce Sullivan, who is writing the new adult literature.

2020 and 2021 have been full of challenges with the presence of Covid-19. However, I am pleased to announce that Zion Assembly Church of God's Sunday School program has forged on and excelled in the face of adversity.

- I have received encouraging reports from Sunday school superintendents who have engaged in outreach activities that not only grew their local Sunday school classes but the church as a whole. Some of the outreach activities included conducting Sunday school in people's homes, having youth activities at the park, hosting vacation Bible school, and celebrating children's day. During quarantine, many leaders taught Sunday school on social media as an outreach tool.

- We have received requests from individuals to be added to our Sunday school email list. We currently have 110 subscribers who are notified when our new lessons are available on the website.

- The Sunday school department is progressing in the development of new Sunday school literature for children, teens, and adults.

We hope to have the new lessons available in January of 2022.

- The offerings received for Sunday school have exceeded last year's offerings. The total amount received for Sunday School this year was $18,45385. These Sunday school offerings help support Zion Assembly's Orphanage Ministries. We currently support 4 orphanages.
  - o Kenya - Brother Wafula
  - o Thailand - Brother Sam Bureenok
  - o India - Brother Padma
  - o Nigeria - Brother Adekunle

I would like to take a moment to recognize our top three churches for excelling in their giving to support Sunday School and the Orphanage Ministries.

1st Place: Greenville, SC - $1,943.50

2nd Place: Cleveland, TN - $1,479.76

3rd Place: West Mobile, AL - $1,368.40

I want to encourage every church to have at least two Sunday school outreach campaigns per year to help boost attendance, and also to remind the Sunday school superintendents of each local church to submit their quarterly reports to headquarters. You can do so by mailing in a written report (the report books are available here at headquarters), or you can submit your report online through our church's website.

Respectfully Submitted
Mandy Thompson
International Sunday School Director

International Shepherding Ministries Report

Greetings to the 18ᵗʰ Annual General Assembly

It is an honor and a privilege to have served as the International Shepherding Ministries Director this year.

During the year, I visited 8 churches and sent three letters to pastors and regional overseers. I attended the office Christmas banquet in Cleveland, TN at the International Headquarters Complex.

I was guest speaker at the International Ladies Retreat in Pigeon Forge, TN. I attended the Regional Ladies Day in West Virgina as well as the post-graduate class of the School of Ministry Institute in Cleveland, TN and the mid-east regional convention in Winchester, Virginia.

I also served as Sunday School Superintendent and Ladies Ministries Director, and taught a Sunday School class and served as worship leader in my local church in Roanoke, Virginia.

My thanks to all the local churches for all that you have done to help raise our Emergency Fund dollars this year, and to Brother Carter, my family, and my local church for their love and support, and especially to Bishop Phillips for having confidence in me to appoint me to this position for the past 5 years.

Respectfully submitted,

Wilma Carter

Shepherding Ministries Director

Assistant Publisher Report

I would like to thank the Lord for the opportunity to serve the church in this position. The printed material is the only way to record accurately, and it is an effective means to impact the world. Through this medium, thoughts and ideas are preserved and made available to others.

After the General Assembly is over, the formatting of the Assembly Minutes begins: records are compiled, edited, and printed. By doing our own publishing, we are able to keep printing costs to a minimum.

I thank the Lord for all that we were able to accomplish this year.

Respectfully Submitted,
Scott E. Neill

Books published
by
Zion Assembly

View of new bookstore

2021 Youth Camp Summary Report

South Central Regional (Camp Revelation)
Directors: Alan and Mandy Thompson
Camp Dates: July 12-16, 2021
Facility/Location: James & Nell Dotson Baptist Campground in Jasper, AL Camp
Theme: "Never Alone" (Is 43.2)
Total Attendance: 42
Camper Attendance: 27
Total Experiences: 2 saved, 3 sanctified, 1 baptized in the Holy Ghost, 1 healed, 16 blessed,
Total Water Baptized: 7

IYC Camper Representatives: Ally Thompson and Parker Harris
IYC Staff Representatives: Hannah Clary and Spencer Plasse

California Camp
Coordinator: Pete Sarry
Camp Date: 6/12/21 One Day Event Facility: Victory Ranch Campground
Theme: Teen camp—"Preeminence of Christ"/ Children's camp— "Build your house upon the rock"
Total attendance: 83
Camper attendance: 63

Tennessee/ Kentucky/ Indiana (Camp Jubilee)
Coordinator: Rick Ferrell
Directors: Travis & Kayla Graves and Kara Spicer Camp Dates: July 19-23, 2021
Facility: Camp Hickory Hills, Dickson, TN Camp Theme: "Fighting the Good Fight" Total Attendance: 90
Camper Attendance: 53
Total Experiences: 6 saved, 11 sanctified, 5 baptized with the Holy

Ghost, 1 divinely healed and 3 called to preach
Total Water Baptized: 8

IYC Camper Representatives: Isaac Dodson, Emma Erwin, and Samuel Fentress IYC Staff Representatives: Alex and Holly Drake

Mid-East Region (Camp Hosanna)

Coordinator: JJ Davis Date· June 21-25, 2021
Facility: Fayette County Campground, Fayetteville, West Virginia.
Total attendance: 100
Camper Attendance: 60
Theme: "Keep Calm & Look Up" with Psalm 30.5 as our theme scripture. Experiences: 20 saved, 14 sanctified
Water Baptized: 17

IYC Camper Representative: Isaac Davis Anita Snyder - Alternate Kiley Preston - Alternate
IYC Staff Representatives: Tyler Smith, Steve and Heather Smith

---

TOTAL CAMP ATTENDANCE: 315
TOTAL CAMPERS: 203

Youth Camp Goal

Zion Assembly youth camps
are driven to save the lost, disciple the saved,
and bring our children and youth together
into the unity of the faith.

Respectfully Submitted,
Kimberly Erwin
Camp Coordinator

School of Ministry Institute Report

It was a privilege to serve the Lord as the director of the School of Ministry Institute (SMI) this year. Along with my responsibilities as SMI director, I also pastored the church in West Pelzer, SC; served as a member of the Executive Council, Chairman of the Doctrine Committee, and also Editor of the Sunday School Literature.

I prepared and preached 93 sermons and taught 45 Bible studies, wrote two new lessons for the school and revised two others. I also taught five classes during SMI and worked together with Bishop Phillips, Wanda Busbee, and Anton Burnette to organize the school in Cleveland. Along with my role as SMI director, I served as Sunday School editor and repurposed lessons for online distribution for adult, teen, and children's classes. Presently, I am working on various kinds of literature for the Sunday School department as well as relevant books and booklets.

The following is my SMI Report. This report only includes the United States schools.

In 2021 two weeks of SMI were conducted in Cleveland, TN

Theme: "A Vision For the Harvest"

Total Students – 58 Full Time Students
1st Week Students: 25
2nd Week Students: 24
Post Grad Students: 20
Auditors: 5
Staff Members: 7
Participants in Church History Tour: 51
SMI Funds received from the Churches and Donations -$5,163.32
Sales of Books -$362
Tuition Received - $6,229
Total Monies Received -$11,754.32
Expenses – $4,701.39
Total Net Income – $7,052.93
Total Expenses to aid the California students - $6,200

These funds were taken from the World Mission Fund. Normally these funds are used annually to bring in overseers to SMI, but since they could not come because of Covid-19, these funds were used to help our students from California attend the Eastern school. This was necessary because of the cancellation of the West Coast school due from Covid 19 restrictions. Part of this money went back into the International Treasury in the form of SMI tuition.

The following is a list of classes taught during the 2 weeks of the Cleveland school:

Week #1 Classes

Disciplined Worship – Anton Burnette

Greek – Wanda Busbee

Kingdom of God and the Church – Wade Phillips

Abstract of the Faith – Bruce Sullivan
    Topics included the Sabbath, Personal Prayer, Personal Bible Study, Church Attendance & Worship, Walking Circumspectly

Abstract of the Faith – Anton Burnette
    Topics included Meats & Drinks, Illicit Relationships, Unequally Yoked, Alcohol and Drugs, Profanity & Swearing, and Worldly Entertainment

Life of Christ – Bruce Sullivan

Spanish (elective) – Renetta Kelton

Week #2 Classes

Disciplined Worship – Anton Burnette

Greek – Wanda Busbee

Abstract of the Faith – Bruce Sullivan
    Topics included Sanctity of Life, Sanctity of the Human Body, Sanctity of Marriage

Glorious Gospel of Christ – Wade Phillips

Holiness History and Doctrine – Bruce Sullivan

Doctrine of the Holy Scriptures – Anton Burnette

I want to thank the following people for making SMI so successful: International Office Staff: Wanda Busbee, Renetta Kelton, Glenda Major, and all who volunteered their time and energy; Instructors: Anton Burnette, Wade Phillips, Wanda Busbee, and Renetta Kelton; the local churches of Cleveland, Tennessee and West Pelzer, South Carolina for cooperating with us [Anton Burnette and me] to take time from our local church responsibilities to teach in these schools; and my wife for her support.

Respectfully submitted
Bruce Sullivan
SMI Director

International Children's Ministries Report

Greetings to the 18th Annual General Assembly

I prepared and organized class materials with the assistance of Lisa Dunn and Grace Burnette. I planned and organized International Children's Day for June and planned the children's program at my local church. I planned and taught with the assistance of Emma Erwin, two classes, and also the Children's Program at the Mid-Central Regional Convention in June. I attended and co-directed with my husband the Junior Camp at Camp Jubilee in July. I planned and organized 7 class sessions and the children's program at the 18th Annual General Assembly. There were 5 teachers and 9 assistants, and a total of 24 children in the class sessions.

Faithfully submitted,
Kayla Graves
Children's Ministry Director

Tract Ministries Report
Greetings to the 18th Annual General Assembly

It has been an exciting year with the opening of the new School of Ministry Institute, the new shower room, and the new book store. It has been thrilling to me and my family to be a small part of the work involved in the fulfillment of these projects. I thank the Lord for all that was accomplished despite losing my my home to a fire and all that was involved in the recovery.

I have recently received a lap top from Headquarters and now have access to the program that would enable me to follow thru with the goal of printing 50 separate tracts. My desire is to receive training on this new program and go to work on them immediately.

To date, I have printed a total of 4,357 tracts. One Thousand, four hundred forty tracts have gone out into the field via our local churches.

I never could have imagined such a fulfilling life as I have had these four years working at headquarters. I am thankful for the opportunity to have worked with the staff and Bishop Phillips this past year.

Respectfully submitted,
Glenda Major
Tract Ministries Director

International Ladies Ministries Report
Greetings to the 18th Annual General Assembly

I wish to thank God for the privilege of serving this year as the Ladies Ministries Director. I give God glory and honor for all that was accomplished. It has been a great blessing to work with the Ladies of Zion.

As Ladies Ministries Director, my primary work for this year was planning and conducting the Regional Ladies Retreats. Because of the COVID pandemic, we were unable to have the Western Region Ladies Retreat. Even though the pandemic was a hindrance, our ladies in this area continued to minister to each other.

On February 26-28, 2021, our Eastern Ladies Retreat was held at Black Fox Lodge in Pigeon Forge, TN. When discussions were being made as to whether we could go ahead with plans to conduct a retreat, it was decided that if we could have around 45 in attendance, it would be possible to proceed and would be a blessing to the small number who could attend. I am so excited to report that despite COVID, we had 70 ladies attend, 18 including first-timers!

Our theme for the retreat was "Flow Through Me Holy Spirit," Scripture reference John 7.37-38: *". . . out of his heart will flow rivers of living water."* Each message, class, and devotion was anointed by the Holy Spirit, and all were refreshed and ready to reach out through evangelism to win lost souls.

In addition to conducting the Ladies Retreat, I attended the Youth Convention held in Cleveland, TN in November. I preached eight messages this year with one receiving salvation. To God be the glory for all that was accomplished.

I want to thank all of our ladies, along with the regional and local leaders and pastors for their support, prayers, and dedication to Ladies Ministries.

Respectfully Submitted,
Pamela Jones
International Ladies Ministries Director

2021 Assembly Business Committee Report

We, your Assembly Business Committee, after prayerful and careful consideration, present this report to the General Assembly for your consideration. Note: This report was accepted unanimously, without dissent.

Section I

Fishing with Jesus

We fully endorse Section I of the Presiding Bishop's 2021 Annual Address, "Fishing with Jesus." Just as Jesus made Peter, Andrew, James and John *"fishers of men"* (Matthew 5:18-22; Luke 5:10), He will make us fishers of men, as well, if we'll obey Him when he says, *"Launch out into the deep and let down our (your) nets for a catch"* (Luke 5:1-8). The effect of their obedience was immediately apparent, *"And when they had done this, they caught a great number of fish . . ."* (Luke 5:9). In addition, to meet the critical need of evangelism, we endorse the creation of the "Department of Evangelism" as a support ministry, led by a director appointed by the Presiding Bishop.

Section II

7 x 70: "The Spirit of Forgiveness"

We fully endorse Section II of the Presiding Bishop's 2021 Annual Address, "7 x 70: The Spirit of Forgiveness." Love and forgiveness, along with all the graces of Christ, must form our corporate personality and the very nature of Zion Assembly, and must be the ruling spirit and principle in our fellowship and all our interactions. As we fulfill our call to be *"fishers of men"* (Matthew 5:18-22), we must allow forgiveness to overrule offenses, hurts, blasphemies, hatefulness, backstabbing, malice, and treachery.

Section III

Importance of Doctrine

We fully endorse Section III of the Presiding Bishop's 2021 Annual Address, "Importance of Doctrine." Biblical doctrine is indispensable, for doctrine informs and trains the conscience in the truths of God and our corporate conscience. The church bears witness to the truth in the Holy Ghost. This doctrine includes the understanding that the church, in union with Christ and one another, is the final arbiter in matters of faith, doctrine, and discipline.

Section IV

Simple Wedding Band

We fully endorse Section IV of the Presiding Bishop's 2021 Annual Address, "Simple Wedding Band." In 2004, the General Assembly unanimously endorsed our stand against the wearing of gold, jewels, pearls, and costly attire, with the exception of the wedding band. It was agreed that a simple wedding band was considered a universal symbol of marriage and in many cases strengthens our strict view of marriage as a sacred institution that is binding until death. Accordingly, we neither encourage nor prohibit the wearing of a simple wedding band, but rather leave it up to the discretion of each couple who are properly married in the eyes of God and the church.

Section V

Financing the Expansion and Development of our International Ministries Complex

We fully endorse Section V of the Presiding Bishop's 2021 Annual Address, "Financing the Expansion and Development of our International Ministries Complex." As we continue to faithfully pay off the existing structure of the International Ministries Complex, we must also turn our attention to the building of the Assembly Tabernacle, which was originally discussed in 2013. The established financial plans, "The King's Plan" and "The Prophet's Plan," which has since been consolidated into the "International Properties Building Fund," has progressed well toward paying off the existing balances. We fully endorse continuing our existing financial plan, while also turning our attention toward raising new funds for the envisioned Assembly Tabernacle.

Section VI

Increase *Voice of Zion* Subscription Rate

As the cost of stamps, printing, handling, and materials increase, we recognize the need to increase the annual rate for the *Voice of Zion*. We recommend an increase of $5.00, from $25.00 annually to $30.00 annually. This change will become effective as of January 1, 2022. Accordingly, SYNC memberships will also increase from $75 annually to $90 annually, and the Lena King club from $250 annually to $300 annually.

Section VII

Endorsement of International Executive Committee

We fully endorse the nominations of the Presiding Bishop to serve with him on the International Executive Council for the 2021-2022 Assembly year: Scott E. Neill, Bruce Sullivan, Joseph A. Steele, Rick Ferrell, L.W. Carter, and Anton Burnette.

Section VIII

Funds

We recommend that we continue to operate the same financial system for this upcoming Assembly year, and that funds be transferred between accounts to bring all funds into a positive balance.

Respectfully submitted,

_____
Zachary Snyder

_____
J.J Davis, Secretary

_____
Kevin Clary

_____
Ricky Graves

_____
Jim Orange

_____
Tod Deakle

_____
Byron Harris

Presiding Bishop's Annual Address

18th Annual General Assembly

August 31-September 5, 2021

Introduction

Much of this annual address focuses on the need for a more robust and thought-through evangelism program in the church. To help get this message across, we have emphasized, "There is no alternative!" to basic outreach, witnessing, personal soul-winning, and revivals conducted by our ministers and local churches. To help enforce this point, I am repeating here what we have emphasized since this great Restoration was launched in 2004, for the message is the very plan that Jesus and the apostles laid out for us in the Scriptures.

If we desire to fulfill the Great Commission that Christ gave to us, there simply is no alternative to "putting boots on the ground" and reaching out to our respective communities, states, nations, and the world at large with the message that Jesus redeems, justifies [saves], sanctifies, and baptizes with the Holy Ghost and fire! (Mt. 3.11; Acts 1.8). We must preach and teach this simple Gospel: that there is a heaven to gain and a hell to shun; that the Gospel gives life over sin and death to whoever will believe and accept it; and that the light of the Gospel is able to overcome and dispel the darkness of evil! That's what the apostle means in saying, *"But we preach Christ and Him crucified and raised from the dead on the third day for our justification"* (Rom. 4.25; 5.18; 1 Cor. 1.30). This is our message: Christ our Redeemer, Deliverer, Healer, and soon coming King! He is also the Head of the church and Savior of the body! This is the Gospel the apostles proclaimed and handed down to us (Acts 2.29-42; Jude 3; 2 Tim. 2.2).

But something is wrong; something is missing among us. We have the message, but do we have the method? Are we hungry for soul-winning evangelism? Are we willing to pay the price to cause revivals to break out among us? Or do we somehow think there is an alternative, or that we can practice a religious routine and somehow fulfill the divine commission?

Let's face the fact, brethren: we are not the spiritual, transforming force in the world that we should be! I recall a saying I heard now and again growing up in West Virginia: "Facts are like mules; they are stubborn things and must be faced." Well, let's face this blatant fact: we must "awake" to the need for outreach and personal witnessing and soul-winning in our churches! According to the prophet, we must *"shake ourselves from the dust"* and not fall back into the mundane and routine (Is. 52.2). Where is the compelling spirit to fill up the House of God with people? Where is our passion for the basic work of the Gospel? Where is the prophetic burden that stirs us to intercede for the lost?Where is the kind of praying that gives new life to sinners? Where are the spiritual conceptions among us that raise dead people [sinners] to newness of life? Where are the sowers who scatter the seeds of the Gospel? Where is He who *"ministereth seed to the sower . . . [multiplies] your seed sown, and [increases] the fruits of your righteousness"* (2 Cor. 9.10; Is. 55.10; Hos. 10.12).

Rachel said, *"Give me children, or else I die."* This must become our desperate cry unto the Lord. Like so many women in the Bible, we must cry out for the Lord to open the womb of Zion! The apostle Paul left us an example of planting spiritual seeds and begetting souls in Christ (1 Cor. 4.15; Gal 4.19; Philem. 10). Like him we must travail until we give birth to sons and daughters in the Lord. Our *"bowels"* [inner man] must be moved (Phil. 1.8; 2.1, 4-5; Philem. 7, 12). We must preach and pray revival down! There is no alternative to personal and corporate [local church] revival! We must make time for it. Whatever it takes, we must beget children, or else: or else we die!

I am reminded here of that remarkable passage in Is. 66.6-9, the essence of which is captured in the sentence *". . . for as soon as Zion travailed, she brought forth her children"* (v. 8). Where are the severe labor pains that precede the bringing forth of new life? Where are the birthing kind of prayers? Where is the intensity of passion needed to convert the lost to Christ? Where is the spirit of conviction? Where are the tears and weeping and the unutterable groanings of the Holy Ghost among us, the kind of prophetic burden and groanings that ignite revival (Jer. 1.9, 18-19; 13.17; 14.17; 31.16-19; Lam. 1.1-6; 2.11, 18)?

> *"Oh, that my head were waters, and mine eyes a fountain of tears, that I might weep day and night for the slain of the daughter of my people!* (Jer. 9.1).

The fact is, brethren, most of our growth since we organized in 2004 took place in the first seven years. In the last few years only three churches and two missions have been set in order in the Unites States, and we are not doing much better in many of the nations where we have established this last days Zion. For the most part, we are not seeing souls saved nor our churches growing! I'm sure you will agree with me when I say, "We must do better, and do more"! More interceding prayers! More outreach! More witnessing! Brethren, we too closely resemble in some ways the lukewarm church at Laodicea (Rev. 3.14-19). May the Lord help us to repent of any laxity and indifference among us and stir us to "awake to righteousness"! Our only recourse for moving forward is an old-fashioned Holy Ghost-anointed and empowered revival!

Section I

"Fishing with Jesus"

> *"So it was, as the multitude pressed about [Jesus] to hear the word of God, that He . . . saw two [boats] standing by the lake . . . Then He got into one of the [boats], which was Simon [Peter's], and . . . said to Simon, 'Launch out into the deep and let down your nets for a catch' . . . And when they had done this, they caught a great number of fish . . . [and] all who were with [Simon] were astonished at the catch they had taken"* (Lk. 5.1-9).

Jesus had the remarkable ability to use illustrations that were familiar to those to whom He was speaking. He thus often used agriculture and the vocation of farming to relate to the people of Palestine, for it was the predominant lifestyle in that region in His day (Mt. 13.1-32, 36-40). Likewise, He often used fishing to relate to the people who lived round about the Sea of Galilee, for fishing was a predominant vocation in that region (Mt. 4.21; Lk. 5.2-6; Jn. 21.6-8). At least seven of the apostles were fishermen, including Peter and Andrew and James and John; thus, He used the metaphor of fishing to teach and train them about evangelizing and winning men to the cause of the Gospel (Mt. 5.18-22; Lk. 5.10).

The chief method of fishing in the Sea of Galilee was boat crews using dragnets (Mt. 4.18-22; Jn. 21.6-8), though fishing with a hook was also a common practice (Mt. 17.27). Several things are worth noting relative to the fishing vocation of the apostles: *First*, it was hard work *("they [had] toiled all night")*, throwing out their nets and pulling them back in again, ofttimes loaded only with sea debris and no fish, as was the case in our text passage (vv. 4-6). In addition, they had to keep their boats and nets mended (Mt. 4.21); attend to their hired help (v. 9), as well as organizing and planning out their fishing schedules.

Jesus related well to hard work, for He Himself was a hard worker both as a carpenter before He began His ministry and afterward in the ministry. Ofttimes in the ministry, He had to go apart to get rest to recuperate from long hours of teaching, being exposed often to the natural elements [heat, rain, cold] beating down upon Him. His praying for the sick was physically draining, and He often walked for miles to preach and meet appointments. He fasted often and prayed earnestly, often for hours calling upon His Father with *"strong crying and tears"* (Heb. 5.7)—even prayed on one occasion until His *"sweat was as it were great drops of blood falling down to the ground"* (Lk. 22.44). Neither did He allow Satan to waste His time away reading the Jerusalem Gazette or listening to the liberal media in Galilee or the latest absurdities coming out of Rome and Babylon. His worldview was not formed by the CNN's and MSNBC's of His day; nor by medical "experts," "scientists," politicians, sociologists, astrophysicists, and religionists. Jesus didn't need therefore to speculate about God and salvation, for He came from the very *"bosom of the Father"* and stayed in communion with Him and His infinite counsel and, accordingly, our Lord knew *"all things"* (Jn. 1.18; 5.20-23; 7.28-29; 14.26; 15.26; 16.13-15).

Second, the fishing business was dangerous work: Storms often suddenly appeared and raged upon the Sea of Galilee, causing ships to sink and the fishermen to drown (Mt. 8.23-27). *Third,* fishing required patience and persistence, for it was difficult to locate the fish and know where to cast the net, and so, accordingly, they just had to kind of "fish around." More than not, professional fishermen drew up empty nets, like the apostles in Lk. 5.5 who had fished all night and had *"taken nothing."* So, the virtue of patience with a fixed determination to keep fishing is a necessary quality for success: You sometimes just have to be persistent and keep trying ["try and try again"] before finally seeing some fruit for your labor. *Fourth,* we must become skillful at fishing, learning, so to speak, the "tricks of the trade." It is said that the best time to fish in the Sea of Galilee is at night. And when fishing in shallow water, the fisherman must be careful not to cast his shadow over the water, for it will frighten the fish away. And, of course, when fishing with a hook it is important to hide the hook with the bait: fish have uncanny survival instincts; remember the old "Charlie Tuna" commercials! So, in that sense fish are not stupid.

When fishing for men, there are "tricks of the trade" and "tools of the trade." *"He that winneth souls is wise"* (Prov. 11.30). We learn how to fish for men from our Lord and the apostles, our elders, and from personal experience. But in any case, the tools of the trade that we learn in the raw must be honed and sharpened to make us more skillful in our task *("iron sharpens iron,"* Prov. 27.17).

Like the fishers of fish, fishers of men must also hide their hook using attractive bait. People are hungry for Good News, but many are leery of false teachers or of being caught in a cult trap. Others are afraid of church government and shy away from anything that smacks of religious duties and responsibilities. To come under church government and Christian responsibilities seem to them to be a hook or net. We must assure them, therefore, that Zion Assembly is interested only in promoting the goodness of God and the furtherance of the Gospel and that there is nothing to fear: in the same way that Jesus assured those who heard Him teach:

> *"If a son shall ask bread of any of you that is a father, will he give him a stone? or if he ask a fish, will he for a fish give him a serpent? Or if he shall ask an egg, will he offer him a scorpion? If ye then, being evil, know how to give good gifts unto your children: how much more shall your heavenly Father give the Holy Spirit to them that ask Him?"* (Lk. 11.11-13)

So, we must seek for wisdom and learn how to make the Gospel appealing and attractive and assure those to whom we witness of the goodness of God and the goodness and harmlessness of our intentions as messengers of Christ. *"Be wise as serpents and harmless as doves"* (Mt. 10.16; see Phil. 2.14-16). Great fishermen ofttimes use flashy bait to attract the fish to the hook or into the net. Our flashy bait in the church is the Good News of the Kingdom of God: eternal life that gives us eternal hope. The hope of the Gospel is attractive and powerful. Think of it: glorified believers shall never die (Jn. 11.26); never get sick or diseased again, never grow old, but will rule and reign with Christ in peace and glory on earth for a thousand years (Rev. 20.3-6); and will dwell forever in heavenly mansions in the holy city, New Jerusalem: and further, finally, inherit a new heaven and new earth wherein dwelleth perfect peace, joy, love, and righteousness forever and forever—a place where there is no more sorrow, heartaches, tears, or pain (Is. 11.1-9; 25.6-9; 35.1-10; 2 Pet. 1.11; Rev. 21.1-5, 9-27; 22.1-5, 14, 17).

Still, no one can preach the Good News of the kingdom without warning sinners of the awful consequences of rejecting Christ or ignoring Him as Lord and Savior. Those who fail to be *"born again [of God]"* (Jn. 1.13; 3.3-8; 1 Pet. 1.23; 1 Jn. 5.1, 4, 18) will surely reap the consequences, namely, the horrors of hell and eternal damnation in the *"lake of fire!"* (Rev. 20.11-15; 21.27; 22.14-15). *"Be not deceived, God is not mocked: whatsoever a man soweth, that shall he also reap"* (Gal. 6.7). Sow to sin and reap its wages—death [spiritual and physical] (Gen. 2.17; Rom. 5.12-14; Heb 9.27) and the *"second death,"* that is, eternal separation from God and all that is good, lovely, blessed, and praiseworthy (Ezek. 18.4; Rev. 20.13-15).

Now observe: Fishing for men is a commandment, a divine commission, not a suggestion or option, that is, if we expect to please God. We must "go fishing" with Him. Listen to the message of God speaking through the prophet: *"Behold, I will send fishers saith the Lord, and they shall fish them . . ."* (Jer. 16.16; see also Heb. 1.14-17). Though this passage is speaking of judgment rather than salvation, the principle is the same metaphorically: God commissions and uses "fishermen" to fulfill His purposes in the earth, including the evangelization of the world. Jesus thus called the apostles into the ministry, saying, *"Follow Me, and I will make you fishers of men,"* for He himself was a fisher of men.

Under another metaphor Jesus says, *"Take My yoke upon you and learn of [or from] Me . . ."* that is, we must get into the harness with

Christ and pull together with Him as oxen that are yoked together to plow and cultivate the ground and reap the harvest. Under still another metaphor, we are called to be like skillful hunters that canvass the mountainsides, diligently looking under every log and in every hole for the prey (Jer. 16.16). Nimrod, the world's first dictator, was a "mighty hunter" before the Lord (Gen. 10.8-9), but he hunted with an evil motive, to satisfy a thirst for temporal power and glory; whereas we hunt with the Lord for souls who will glorify the Lord and accept Christ as their Lord and Savior.

Get Jesus in the Boat with You

We have noticed the encouraging promise that Jesus will go fishing with us. That makes us *"laborers together with [Him]"* in the great enterprise of fishing for men. He got into the boat with Peter and Andrew, and at His command the boat was launched out into the deep. The fishermen had been on the land with Him, now He is in the sea with them. They had attended upon Him in His preaching, He is now accompanying them in their fishing.

Jesus adds a supernatural dimension to our fishing. He knows where the fish are, and has the authority to call fish into the net or to the hook; or is it that He creates fish ["new creatures," 1 Cor. 5.17] to fulfill His eternal purpose? In the account in Luke 5.8-10, we see a miraculous demonstration of His omnipotence and omniscience at work. Did He know where the fish were and called them into the net to enlarge His kingdom (Mt. 13.47-48; Lk. 14.21-23)? or was it that He created the fish for that purpose? Was it a school of fish in one place, and the fish came together at His call? Or were they each [all 153 of them—Jn. 21.11] isolated and came together at His will from every direction to meet at that precise spot and that precise moment? And if He knows the number of the stars and calls them each by its name, billions of them (Ps. 147.4), did He call all these fish each by its name?

"Great is the Lord, and of great power;
His understanding is infinite (Ps. 147.5)

66

We see the same kind of glorious miracle in the arrangement Jesus made for His and Peter's payment of their temple tax. He sent Peter to the sea, to the very fish that had a coin ["a piece of money"] in its mouth, sufficient to pay the exact amount of their taxes (Mt. 17.27). Did He put the coin at that moment in the fish's mouth, or had the fish swallowed the coin days or even months before; and the Lord, foreseeing the need and the unfolding of the whole scenario of events, ordained that that peculiar fish would swallow the hook that Peter cast into the sea *("the fish that first cometh up")*? Was it mere happenstance that Peter went exactly to the spot by the water's edge to meet that one fish? No, everything suggests it was a divine appointment. Think of it! Of all the billions of fish in the sea, that one especially found its way to the very spot where it would meet Peter. Did the fish find Peter or did Peter find the fish? Did the Lord order the fish to be there [omnipotence] or did He just know [omniscience] that it would be there? Or, yet again, did He create the fish for this special purpose? Or, still again, did He create the coin and omnipotently place it in the fish's mouth at the very moment that Peter hooked it?

These same questions arise when we study Jonah and the *"great fish"* that swallowed him [probably a whale or perhaps the remnant of a species of aquatic-land dinosaur [Job 40.15–41.1-2, 15-34; Ps. 74.13-14; Is. 27.1]; or is it possible that it was a unique creature that God formed for that special purpose? Whatever the nature of the miracle, the Word says that God had *"prepared a great fish"* to swallow the disobedient and angry prophet (Jonah 1.17) to teach him a great lesson about evangelizing the world; to save him from drowning; and to prefigure the resurrection of Christ (Mt. 12.40). But not only had the Lord prepared a great fish for that occasion, He *"prepared a gourd and made it come up over Jonah"* for shade and comfort (4.6) but He also *"prepared a worm"* to destroy the gourd the next day (v. 7), and then *"prepared a vehement [hot] east wind"* (v. 8) all of which to chastise, teach, and train Jonah of God's grace and missionary purpose, and the nature of his own calling. So, however one may interpret the peculiar workings of all these mysteries, they were written for our learning (Rom. 15.4; 1 Cor.

9.10; 10.11) to teach us that the Lord Jesus has the whole world in His hands, and that His knowledge, wisdom, and redeeming power are infinite.

Now why would anyone doubt Jesus' power to perform any of the miracles recorded in the Scriptures? He made a rooster [a "birdbrain"] to crow on cue (Jn. 13.38; Mt. 26.74); commanded ravens [vicious birds of prey] to feed a prophet when the bird's instinct was to eat the prophet, not feed him (1 Kg. 17.4-6). He enabled an ass [donkey] to speak the Word of God in Hebrew or Aramaic to rebuke a false prophet (Num. 22.28-30; 2 Pet. 2.16); caused cows to leave their nursing calves crying for their mothers' milk to identify His people and prove His sovereignty (1 Sam. 6.7-12). He *"stopped the mouths of lions"* (Judg. 14.5-6; 1 Sam. 17.34-36; Dan. 6.22; Heb. 11.33); enabled His people to destroy whole nations with hornets (Deut. 7.17-24; Joh. 24.12).

What more could be said: He's the One who parted the Red Sea; caused the waters of Jordan to stand up and salute the power of God! He intervened for the widow of Zarephath, supernaturally filling her barrel with meal [flour] and her small jar of oil to the brim, keeping both miraculously resupplied (1 Kg. 17.12-16); then He raised the widow's son from the dead (vv. 17-22). He spoke and cured Naaman of leprosy (2 Kg. 5.3-14), then passed on Naaman's leprosy to Gehazi, a servant of Naaman who had become deceitful and greedy (vv. 20-27); and purified the pot of poisoned stew so that Elisha and his school of prophets could eat (4.38-41). In all these instances, Elijah and Elisha were instruments for the working of miracles, but it was Jesus who provided the supernatural power!

This same Jesus turned water into wine [changed its chemical nature]; caused a river to flow out of a rock to quench the thirst of 2-3 million of His people in the *"church in the wilderness"* (Ex. 17.6; Ps. 105.41; 1 Cor. 10.4); made bread [*"angel's food"*] fall from heaven like rain (Ps. 105.40); caused a wind to blow in from the sea that brought quail enough to feed millions of His people at one time (Num. 11.31-32; Ps. 105.40): and on another occasion fed 10-20 thousand people with two fish and five loaves of bread (Mt. 14.15-21); He opened deaf ears; made the blind to see; the lame to walk; the mute to speak, and on another occasion muted His own people who doubted His Word (Lk. 1.5-6, 20). And there is still more that could be said to show forth His glory and prove that He can use us to fill His house with people and fulfill our mission. This is His will: that we should reach out by faith and diligently labor to spread the Gospel, compelling all to come *". . . that My house may be filled"* (Lk. 14.23).

Now if the Lord can cause gourds, and worms, and roosters, and donkeys, and birds, and lions and fish and the weather and the whole order of the cosmos to obey Him, then, surely, He can help us fill our boats with fish and our churches with people. If He can walk on water and enable Peter to do the same, He can do anything! How wonderful it is that He is willing to go fishing with us, to enable us to fulfill His will and purpose through the church! He promises us that we will *"catch men"* if we are persistent and compelling in our witnessing.

What's Missing?

Since we are assured in the prophetic Word that we will at last succeed in our mission, why are we not presently realizing more growth? What is lacking on our part? We have the message, the capability, the spiritual gifts, the power [delegated authority and dynamic power], the organization [support ministries], the anointing, and the divine commission to evangelize the world: see Acts 1.8: starting at *"Jerusalem"* [our local cities and communities] then *"all Judea and Samaria"* [our states and regions], and *"the uttermost part of the earth"* (Acts 1.8). And Jesus has promised, *"lo, I am with you always, even unto the end of the world."*

Then what is missing for us to realize a greater increase in our fishing enterprise? For one thing our "willingness" to get up and get out to do the work. See, we not only need Jesus in the boat with us: we need to put our boats in the water—to launch out into deep at His command! For God will not take over and do what He has called us to do. He glories in us being *"laborers together with Him." "[We] are God's husbandry"* (1 Cor. 3.9). Have you noticed this in the area where you live? We need churches in every city and town in the world, but where are they? God sees the need, but He is not doing the work that He has assigned us to do (Mt. 28.19-20; Mk. 16.16-17).

Regarding our part of the work in laboring together with God: Solomon and the building of the temple serve to illustrate this truth. Listen to David's advice to him:

> *"And thou Solomon my son . . . serve Him with a perfect heart and with a willing mind . . . Take heed now; for the LORD hath chosen thee to build a house for the sanctuary: be strong and do it"* *(1 Chron. 28.9-10).*

A little later David spoke in the same fashion to the whole congregation of Israel, saying,

> *"And who then is willing to consecrate his service to the LORD? Then the chief of the fathers and princes of the tribes of Israel, and the captains of thousands and of hundreds, with the rulers of the king's work, offered willingly" (29.5-6).*

We find this same willing spirit in the rebuilding of God's house after the Babylonian Captivity, a principle that is carried forward in the New Testament in the building of God's house under the terms of the New Covenant. The apostle Paul magnified this willing spirit among the saints in Macedonia, noting that they gave *"willingly of themselves"* according to the *"will of God"* (2 Cor. 8.3, 5). Then Paul urges the Corinthians to do the same. They had promised to support the work, but had not fulfilled their commitment; and thus, the apostle now urges them to *"perform the doing of it"* of what they had promised, saying, *". . . that as there was a readiness to will, so there may be a performance also . . ."* (vv. 10-12).

Now this is true not only regarding money, but of giving of our time and labor and energy to the Lord. We should so love the LORD and be so zealous for the house of God that we will willingly lay aside every weight to put Him and the work of the church first in our lives (Mt. 6.33; Mk. 10.29-30)—all of us engaging willingly in doing *"the work of an evangelist."* Finally, we have the prophetic promise that in these very last days, God will raise up a people who will lay aside the allure of temporal riches and pleasures to put Christ and the Gospel and His church first above all! Listen to the prophet:

> *"Thy people shall be willing in the day of thy power, in the beauties of holiness . . ." (Ps 110.3).*

Secondly, we need people skills to fulfill the mission. We noted above we have the capability, but we need the ability [skills] and wisdom. For *"He that winneth souls is wise"* (Prov. 11.30). We must learn how to approach people and how to become *"all things to all men that [we] might by all means save some"* (1 Cor. 9.19, 22). No doubt this is partly what Jesus meant when He said, *"For the children of this world are wiser in their generation than the children of light"* (Lk. 16.8), namely, the children of this world often demonstrate more effective people skills and more ability to manage money and attract people. May the Lord teach us how to be good stewards of our time and energy, as well as our finances for the edification of the church and the glory of God.

Yet there is still something more important that needs again to be emphasized here: WE NEED CHRIST IN THE BOAT WITH US! We have seen His wonders and miracle-working power, and His willingness to go fishing with us. We have His promise that if we become *"laborers together with Him,"* we will realize increases in everything—numbers, finances, and spirituality. We may rest assured that He will show us where to cast our nets and enable us to enclose 153 great fish and many more, because He said,

> *"He that believeth on me, the works that I do shall he do also; and greater works than these shall he do; because I go to the Father" (Jn. 14.12-13).*

Fishing Indiscriminately

One final thing should be said regarding this subject. We are commanded to fish for men indiscriminately. This is one of the main lessons in Jesus' parable of the Dragnet in Mt. 13.47-48. The same is true in His parable of the Wedding Banquet in 22.1-14, see esp. vv. 10-12. For the Gospel is open to all—to everyone in every tribe, race, nation, and tongue (Is. 49.6; 60.1-10; Acts 15.16-17). See, *"The Lord is . . . not willing that any should perish, but that all should come to repentance"* (2 Pt. 3.9); and again: *"whosoever will [let him come] and take of the water of life freely"* (Rev. 22.17). The evangelistic principle is this: *". . . whosoever shall call upon the Lord shall be saved"* (Acts 2.21; Rom. 10.13).

Lest there be any confusion in the meaning of these two parables, Jesus concludes the Wedding Banquet parable, saying, *"For many are called but few are chosen"* (v.14). The Gospel was presented first to the Jews who were heirs of the kingdom of God, but they rejected Christ as the Messiah and His right and power to save on the terms of the New Covenant (Mt. 3.10-12; 10. 5-8; 21.33-44; Lk. 19.14; Jn. 1.11-12; Rom. 2.28-29; 10.1-4; 11.20-23). The Jews as a nation rejected the Gospel, even as they do now, and for this same reason, the Lord opened the wedding feast to all the children of men indiscriminately (Lk. 14.15-24). *"Whosoever will let him come!"* But now observe, only those who truly repented and bore the fruit of salvation and were properly dressed for the occasion remained part of the wedding party. The same is true for this present generation. Our Great Commission commands us to preach the Gospel to every creature, but also that we should baptize and add to the church only those who truly repent, believe the Gospel, and bear the fruit of holiness (Mt. 28.19-20; Mk. 16.15-16; Lk. 13.3, 5; Jn. 3.3-8; Acts 2. 36-42; Rom. 6.19-22; 1 Cor. 6.9-11; Heb. 12.14).

We have stressed the point that there is no alternative to fulfilling our mission than returning to the basics of evangelism. Let us fix in our minds and spirit therefore to leave this Assembly with the aim and commitment to go into the *"streets and lanes of the city"* and in *"the highways and hedges"* of the countryside and *"compel [the people]"* to come in (Lk. 14.21-23). But also, to realize increases and to succeed, we must get Jesus in the boat with us, launch out into the deep, and fish with Him!

Finally, brethren, this ministry is so important and demanding at this juncture on our journey, that it would be helpful, it seems to me, to organize and incorporate it as a support ministry with a director. This would keep the subject and need of evangelism ever before us. It would be no less than a restoration of the Department of Evangelism that we had in our former fellowship years ago. If this seems wise to the members of the ABC, a recommendation may be brought before the Assembly for consideration.

Section II
7 x 70
"The Spirit of Forgiveness"

[Note, Section I of the Annual Address was featured
in the September issue of the *Voice of Zion*].

The ground of brotherly love and forgiveness, and even the capacity to love and forgive our enemies, is found in God himself. It is the nature of God to want to forgive and reconcile sinners on the basis of His love and truth (Jn. 3.16; Rom. 3.24-26; 1 Cor. 5.18-20; Eph. 2.8; 2 Pet. 3.9). Likewise, it is the nature of the saints of God to desire to forgive and reconcile on that same basis. For *"God is love"* and the spiritual DNA of God is written in the hearts of believers who are "born of God" (Jn. 3.5-8; Pet. 1.23; 1 Jn. 3.9; 5.18; see also Jer. 24.7; 31.33; 32.40; Ezek. 11. 19-21; 36. 26-27; 2 Cor. 3.2-3; Heb. 8.10). *"If any man be in Christ, he is a new creature [or creation]"* (2 Cor. 5.17); reborn ["born again"] in the image of Christ (Jn. 3.3-8; 2 Cor. 3.18; Eph. 2.10; Col. 3.10; 4.24). In and through the Holy Spirit, the very seed of God in Christ is infused

73

into our being: so that we have the very nature of God within us, that is, we are *"partakers of the divine nature"* (1 Pet. 1.4); *"being born again, not of corruptible seed, but of the incorruptible, by the word of God, which [lives and abides] forever"* (1 Pet. 1.23; see also Gal. 3.16, 29).

This is the reason that failure to forgive is unforgivable: it indicates the absence of the Holy Spirit and a heart that has not been cleansed.

"And when ye stand praying, forgive, if ye have aught against any: that your Father also which is in heaven may forgive you your trespasses. But if ye do not forgive, neither will your Father which is in heaven forgive your trespasses" (Mk. 11.25-26; see also Mt. 6.12, 14-15; Lk. 11.4).

This is what Peter failed to perfectly grasp while his mind was still being influenced by the law and ancient traditions. He was looking at things from a legal or forensic standpoint rather than through the lens of the Gospel with its inward grace and power. He saw forgiveness as something exacted and calculated, requiring a formal meeting between the offender and the one offended. He thus asked Jesus, *"Lord, how oft shall my brother sin against me, and I forgive him? Till seven times?"* Jesus said, *"I say not unto thee, Until seven times: but, Until seventy times seven"* (Mt. 18.21-22; Lk. 17.4). The LORD makes this perfectly clear in the parable of the wicked servant who, after being forgiven by his Master, refused to forgive one of his fellow servants his debt, and even had him thrown into prison. This angered the Master and He *"delivered him to the tormentors"* (vv. 23-34). Jesus said, *"So likewise shall my heavenly Father do also unto you, if ye from your hearts forgive not everyone his brother their trespasses"* (v. 35). The key point to grasp is *"... if ye from your hearts forgive not."*

There is of course a forensic or judicial aspect to settling issues and arguments in the church (Mt. 18.15-18; Jn. 20.23). Primarily, however, the individual member is responsible to go to his brother to resolve differences and restore peace and harmony (Mt. 5.23-24;

74

18.15; Lk. 17.3-4; et al). Resolving issues and differences brings closure and helps to avoid conflict and further misunderstandings. Still, differences and offenses cannot be settled to the LORD's pleasing except in sincerity and from the heart: for unlike carnal men who judge according to the outward appearance, God sees into the heart, and judges accordingly (1 Sam. 16.7; 1 Kg. 8.39; Ps. 7.9; Jer. 11.20; 17.10; Acts 1.24; Rev. 2.9, 13, 19).

True forgiveness, fellowship, and spiritual unity in the church can only be realized as it flows from the heart, for *"out of the heart proceed . . . the issues of life"* (Prov. 4.23; Mt. 15.18-19; Mk. 7.18-23). Recall that this practice was the hypocrisy of the scribes and Pharisees: Jesus said they were *"like [whitewashed tombs] that appear beautiful outward, but are within full of dead men's bones, and of all uncleanness"* (Mt. 23.27).

Forgiveness is better caught than taught; it is something to be experienced as well as to be learned. Its source is the Holy Spirit Himself. It is therefore a spirit as well as a principle—a spirit that must fill our hearts as well as our minds and lips. See, unforgiveness not only provokes God to wrath, it is self-destructive; it is a spirit that poisons the soul!

God's forgiveness is unfathomable and inexplicable, so gracious that mortal minds cannot comprehend, nor mortal words explain it. For who can fully understand and explain God's love and desire to forgive and reconcile Himself with fallen humanity, especially at the expense of the suffering and death of His *"only begotten Son"*? Who can explain that His holiness requires Him to separate Himself from sinners, yet His love works to reconcile them through faith and repentance? For *"faith . . . worketh by love"* (Gal. 5.6). We can only proclaim, like the apostle John, the glorious truth of the matter: *"God so loved the world . . . [that is, His love so moved Him, that it] "pleased the Lord to bruise [His Son] . . . [to] put Jesus to grief [and make His] soul an offering for sin"* (Is. 53.10).

"Could we with ink the ocean fill,
And were the skies of parchment made;
Were every stalk on earth a quill,
And every man a scribe by trade;

To write the love of God above
Would drain the oceans dry;
Nor could the scroll contain the whole,
Though stretched from sky to sky.

"O love of God, how sweet and pure!
How measureless and strong!
It shall forevermore endure—
The saints' and angels' song"

The commandment to love our enemies can be fulfilled only by one who has been reborn in the image of Christ. The gift of love *[agape]* gives the believer the grace and power to *"Love your enemies, bless them that curse you, do good to them that hate you, and pray for them which despitefully use you, and persecute you"* (Mt. 5.44). It is the kind of love that says, even while your enemies are crucifying you, *"Father forgive them; for they know not what they do"* (Lk. 23.34); the kind of love that moved Christ, yea compelled Him to die for us, even while we were yet sinners (Rom. 5.8).

The commandment to love one's enemies is not new: read Ex. 23.4-5; Prov. 24.17; 25.21). In Rom. 12.20 the apostle quotes Prov. 25.21 to support his admonition to love one's enemies. It is thus not a new commandment because it is the same eternal, unchangeable God who commanded it under the Old Covenant (1 Jn. 2.7-8)! The seeming contradiction in Jesus' words in Jn. 13.34, in which He says that the command *"to love one another"* is a *"new commandment,"* is speaking of loving under the terms of the New Covenant in Christ, that is, of God's love that now indwells our hearts by the transforming power of the Holy Spirit. The key distinction in the *"new commandment"* is to love one another *"as I [Jesus] have loved you."* That is what is new: an inward transformation, the heart of God within us, infused grace, and the Spirit of forgiveness! As such, we now have a readiness and inclination to forgive, for God's love requires it (1 Cor. 13.4-8, 13).

The impartation of God's love in our hearts is the free gift of His grace working through faith, making us able and willing to obey His law (Rom. 5.18-21; Eph. 2.8). It is not therefore the result of any inherent or innate goodness of our own, but rather love and goodness which is *"spread abroad in our hearts by the Holy Ghost which is given unto us"* (Rom. 5.5). As such, this kind of love *[agape]* is not just a discipline or effort to bring about civility and the pretense of peace, but the very act of God working supernaturally to infuse into our hearts His grace and moral power.

> "O love of God, how sweet and pure . . .
> Redeeming grace to Adam's race"

Agape is especially manifested in brotherly love and kindness, in the lives of those whose *"hearts [are] knit together in love"* (Col. 2.2, 19), and more especially in the saints who make up the *"household of God"* (Gal. 6.10; Eph. 2.19; 3.15; 4.16). For *"if we cannot love our brother whom we have seen, how can we love God whom we have not seen"* (1 Jn. 4.20; 5.1). The love of God is the *"bond of perfectness"* (Col. 3.14), and therefore should be encouraged and cultivated all the more in the church. Now let the words of the apostle sink down into your ears: *"Let love be without dissimulation"* [without hypocrisy or discord]. *"Abhor that which is evil; cleave to that which is good. Be kindly affectioned one to another with brotherly love; in honor preferring one another"* (Rom. 12.9-10; 1 Tim. 1.5-6; 1 Pet.1.22).

This is the key to understand the command to forgive our enemies and those who persecute and despitefully use us, and also to forgive our brothers and sisters in Christ who may offend ["scandalize"] us. For the spirit of forgiveness dwells in the hearts of those who have been reborn in the image of Christ [not should dwell but does indeed dwell]! The spirit or forgiveness is as much the fruit of the Spirit as love, joy, peace, faith, longsuffering, and goodness. It is a sign of salvation more so than baptism or eating at the Lord's Table, for it comes from the heart of one who has been born again in the image of Christ.

The very core of *agape* produces the ***"fruit of the Spirit"***—love, joy, peace, longsuffering, gentleness, goodness, faith, meekness, temperance (Gal. 5.22-25); all aspects of which, if lived out, show proof that our ***"old man"*** is crucified with Christ and that we have ***"put on the new man, which after God is created in righteousness and true holiness"*** (Eph. 4.24). We are accordingly admonished to cultivate all these graces in the life of the church (Rom. 6.4-13, 18-22), that is, to ***"walk in the Spirit,"*** be ***"led of the Spirit,"*** and to ***"live in the Spirit"*** (Gal 5. 16, 18, 25); for in so doing we show forth the grace of Christ, and as such, ***"... make all men see what is the fellowship of the mystery . . .,"*** that is, we become on earth the visible and tangible embodiment and revelation of the ascended Christ (2 Cor. 3-2; Eph. 3.9-10; Jn. 13.35; 1 Pet. 2.9; see also Is. 49.1-7; 52.1-2, 7-10; 54. 1-10; 60.1-14). Being under the New Covenant, we visibly embody also the fruit of the Spirit, that is, we are ***"an habitation of God thru the Spirit,"*** ***"a temple in the Lord"*** (1 Cor. 3.17; 2 Cor. 6.16; Eph. 2.21-22).

It is difficult to grasp the grace and glory that is bestowed upon the church, for we are His ambassadors, and as such, are ordained and anointed to pray and admonish in ***"Christ's stead"*** (2 Cor. 5.20); as well as to love and forgive and minister in Christ's stead (Lk. 19.13; 2 Cor. 5.18-21).

> "Out in the highways and byways of life,
> Many are weary and sad;
> Carry the sunshine where darkness is rife,
> Making the sorrowing glad.
>
> Make me a blessing, Make me a blessing,
> Out of my life may Jesus shine;
> Make me a blessing, O Savior, I pray,
> Make me a blessing to someone today."

Our call and mission is therefore not only to reach the lost, but to be the corporate personality of Christ in this world and to cultivate His disposition in the life of the church; so that *"we all, with open face beholding as in a glass the glory of the Lord, are changed into the same image from glory to glory, even as by the Spirit of the Lord"* (2 Cor. 3.18).

Now we have focused on forgiveness to explain the broader aspects of grace; namely, that all the graces of the Spirit should permeate our fellowship and rule and reign in our lives and in the corporate life of the church. Graces such as humility, mercy, kindness, tenderheartedness, goodness, thankfulness, and forbearance must be our rule of faith and practice. For this was the doctrine and practice of Christ and the apostles, and we are building upon that foundation (Acts 2.42; Eph. 2.20-22). These graces fill the pages of the New Testament. They form the light that radiates from God's church in a dark world. Holiness and all the graces of the Spirit should therefore penetrate the very soul of the church and flow freely out from us to a world bound by sin and iniquity.

> *"Walk in wisdom toward them that are without, redeeming the time. Let your speech be always seasoned with salt, that ye may know how ye ought to answer every man"* *(Col. 4.5-6).*

> *"Let your loins be girded about, and your lights burning; And ye yourselves like unto men that wait for their Lord . . ." (Lk. 12.35).*

> *"That ye may be blameless and harmless, the sons of God, without rebuke, in the midst of a crooked and perverse nation, among whom ye shine as lights in the world"* *(Phil. 2.15)*

But now observe: These graces also build up the church and enrich our fellowship and interrelationships. Jesus, Paul, and all the inspired writers of the New Testament encourage and admonish us to "let" these graces rule in the church and permeate us through and through!

79

"Be ye therefore followers of God, as dear children; And walk in love, as Christ also hath loved us, and hath given himself for us an offering and a sacrifice to God for a sweetsmelling savour" (Eph. 5.1-2).

"Wherefore be ye not unwise, but understanding what the will of the Lord is. And . . . be filled with the Spirit; Speaking to yourselves in psalms and hymns and spiritual songs, singing and making a melody in your heart to the Lord; Giving thanks always for all things unto God and the Father in the name of the Lord Jesus Christ" (vv. 17-20).

"Let no corrupt communication proceed out of your mouth, but that which is good to the use of edifying, that it may minister grace unto the hearers. And grieve not the Holy Spirit of God . . . Let all bitterness, and wrath, and anger, and clamor, and evil speaking, be put away from you, with all malice: And be ye kind one to another, tenderhearted, forgiving one another, even as God for Christ's sake hath forgiven you" (Eph. 4.29-32).

We see then there are things to *"put on"* and things to *"put off"* (Col. 3.8-14). The apostle's reasoning is that since we have *"put off the old man with his deeds"* and *"have put on the new man, which is renewed in knowledge after the image of him that created him,"* we should live up to our testimony and not frustrate the grace of Christ!

The things we are admonished to put off are these: "fornication," "uncleanness," "inordinate affections," "evil concupiscence," "lying," "anger," "wrath," "malice," "blasphemy," "filthy communication out of your mouth" (vv. 5-9). The things we are admonished to put on are these: "bowels of mercies," "kindness," "humbleness of mind," "meekness," "longsuffering," "forbearance of one another," "forgiveness," "peace," and "charity *[agape]*" (vv. 12-15).

It follows then that we should *put on* courteousness and hospitality (1 Pet. 3.8; Acts 28.7-10; 1 Tim. 3.2-3) with cheerfulness (Rom. 12.8; 2 Cor. 9.7) and *put off* clamor, anger, unruliness, and any trace of a superior or haughty disposition (Eph. 4.31; Prov. 15.1-2, 13); for we are what we are by the grace of God! If we let Him, the Spirit of grace will perfect us individually and corporately as the body of Christ (1 Cor. 7.1-2; Eph. 5.26-27).

Notice how many times we are admonished to "let" these graces abound in our lives and interaction with others. This is because we remain, even after we are regenerated and sanctified, free moral agents and subject to be tempted and to fall back into an unruly and carnal disposition. We are therefore admonished by Peter and Jude, the Lord's brother, to keep up our prayer life and consecration, so to *"make [our] calling and election sure"* and to *"keep us from falling"* (2 Pet. 1.4-13; Jude 24-25). Paul also warns believers to give heed always, lest one fall from grace and come again under condemnation (1 Cor. 10.11-12; Phil. 4.1; 1 Thess. 3.8; Heb. 4.11; et al).

Listen to the apostle's further admonition: *"let the peace of God rule in your hearts, to the which also ye are called in one body; and be ye thankful"* (Col. 3.15). It is a principle which is applicable to all the graces of the Spirit; that is, we must *"let"* them rule: let love rule; let forgiveness rule; let thankfulness rule; let mercy rule; let gentleness rule; let goodness rule; let joy rule; let tenderheartedness rule; let faith rule; let kindness rule!

I am challenging us to let love and forgiveness and all the graces of Christ form our corporate personality and the very nature of Zion Assembly; let all these graces be the ruling spirit and principle in our fellowship and our interactions with others. Let forgiveness overrule offenses [scandalous accusations and gossip], hurts, blasphemies, hatefulness, backstabbing, malice, and treachery. Let our hearts be filled with the Holy Spirit, and there will be no room for bitterness, hateful arguments, carnal debates, variance, schisms, seditions, and the *"works of the flesh."* Let 7x70 be the basis for all the graces of Christ to work in our fellowship and outreach to others. Let

81

mercies prevail over and over against judgment. Let kindness and tenderheartedness be the rule of the church. Above all, let holiness and love prevail evermore, for this is the *"more excellent way"*!

Finally, to help us be mindful of our spiritual responsibilities and moral obligations regarding the graces of Christ and our fellowship in Him (2 Pet. 1. 5-8, 12-13; 3.1-2), we have designed a pin to display on the lapels of our jackets and suits or on our shirts and blouses. It represents the spirit as well as the principle of forgiveness and all the graces of God in Christ. The pin often opens also the door for us to witness to others about our blessed Savior, for many will ask what the pin signifies. I wore one of the 7x70 pins recently, and the curiosity of several people caused them to enquire as to its meaning which gave me the opportunity to witness to them.

There are two designs of the pin, slightly different, from which to choose. They are available in the bookstore and gift shop for $3.99, or can be ordered by writing to Glenda Major, P.O. Box 2398, Cleveland, TN 37323 or calling (423)-476-3337. I want to encourage all our ministers and members to make good use of this plan for outreach and church growth. These pins also make great gifts for friends and family.

Section III
"Importance of Doctrine"

There is nothing plainer or more emphatically stated in the Scriptures than the importance and indispensability of doctrine. Jesus said,

> *". . . My doctrine is not mine, but His that sent me. If any man will do His will he shall know of the doctrine, whether it be of God, or whether I speak of myself"* (Jn. 7.16-17).

Anticipating his impending martyrdom, the apostle Paul wrote to Timothy,

> *"Take heed unto thyself, and unto the doctrine; continue in them: for in doing this thou shalt both save thyself, and them that hear thee"* (1 Tim. 4.16).

And it is said of the whole church in the New Testament,

> *". . . they continued steadfastly in the apostles' doctrine and fellowship . . ."* (Acts 2.42).

All of Jesus' and apostles' teachings compose "the doctrine" of the church. Note Paul's words carefully: *"Take heed . . . unto the doctrine; continue in them . . ."* We see in this admonition that the doctrine of Christ is composed of many doctrines, all of which are important and necessary to observe (Mt. 4.4; 5.19-20; 28.19-20; Acts 20.20, 27; Eph. 5.27; 2 Thess. 2.13-17; 1 Tim. 4.6-7; Rev. 22.18-19).

There are literally scores of passages that emphasize the importance of doctrine. Yet a common deception among "Christian" ministers and churches today is that doctrine is not so important. They even say absurd things such as "doctrines corrupt," "doctrines are legalistic," "doctrines hinder the work of the Holy Spirit," etc. A belief held in common by many is that love and mercy trump doctrine, as if love and mercy were not part of the doctrine.

There is a movement still with us today that became popular in the 1880s that fosters the idea, "In essentials unity, in non-essentials liberty, in all things charity." Those who advocate this idea insist that it promotes Christian brotherhood and unity: but, upon close examination, it is rather a bankrupt ideal. For it is impossible to have Christian unity except on the terms of Jesus' and the apostles' teachings—all of them! (Jn. 17.6, 8, 14, 20-23; Eph. 2.20; 4.11-16; 2 Pet. 2.1-3). In this sense doctrines do indeed divide, and so they should; they divide the sincere from the pretentious; the reverent from the foolish; the true from the false; the devout and saintly from the superficial; Godly and upright men from deceivers and false teachers; honest men from pernicious men; sober-minded men and women of God from giddy, flaky pretenders; men with gravity and eldership from lightweights and novices (Mt. 5.18-20; 10.34-39; 13.21-22; 1 Cor. 11.18-19; 2 Pet 2.1-3; Rev. 22.18-19)!

Those who hold to the theological formula mentioned above seem to think they can negotiate their own standard of faith and practice; that is, form their own body of doctrine and creedal statement or so-called declaration of faith. It reminds us of Jesus' criticism of the Pharisees who supplanted the doctrine of God with their own doctrines and traditions, *"making the word of God of [no] effect"* (Mt. 15.3-9; Mk. 7.7-9, 13; see also Jer. 7.23-24; Is. 24.4-5). But see, "the doctrine" belongs to God (Jn. 7.16; 8.28-32, 47; 12.49-50); it was settled in Heaven in eternity and laid out for us in the Holy Scriptures (Ps. 119.89, 152; Lk. 21.33; 16.12-15; 2 Tim. 3.15-16: 2 Pet. 1.19-21). Our calling is simply to adjudicate according to the Word of God, not legislate; that is, we interpret God's law; we do not make laws!

The idea of building a "church without walls" is being advocated by many today; but the very purpose of the Bible church is to build walls between truth and error, between sinners and saints, between right and wrong, between light and darkness. The Lord's Zion, the City of God, has walls, just like it has "foundations!" (Ps. 48.11-13; Ezra. 9.9; Neh. 1.3-4; 2.17; Is. 60.14; Lk. 6.48-49; Eph.2.20; Rev. 21.14, 18-19). A church without foundations and walls is no church at all! For the church is by its very nature a visible structure of government and discipline, a fellowship of concrete teachings (Mt. 16.18-19; 18.15-20); a body ruled by governors and elders (Acts 15. 2, 4, 6, 22-28; 20.28; Titus 1.5; Heb. 13.7, 17).

"Walls" are intended to protect those within the house of God and prevent false brethren, false teachers, hypocrites, and heretics from entering—though a "creep" here and there may yet manage to enter "unaware" (Gal. 2.4; Jude 3). No, it is not the walls of the church that divide sincere believers: it is rather the lack of walls and, more to the point, it is sin and carnality [the "flesh"] that separate [divide] sincere believers from God and other believers. Hear the prophet: *"These are they who separate themselves, sensual, having not the Spirit"* (Jude 19), and again, *"They went out from us, but they were not of us: for if they had been of us, they would no doubt have continued with us: but they went out, that they might be made manifest that they were not of us"* **(1 Jn. 2.19).** Paul in no uncertain terms identifies "strife," "sedition" "schism," and "heresies" as "works of the flesh" (Rom. 12.16; 15.5-6; 1 Cor. 1.10-11; Gal. 5.20; Phil 3.16). Divisions and the scattering of God's people have been caused by slander, malicious gossip, evil speaking, contentiousness, self-conceit, headiness, unruliness, and puffed-up novice preachers who *"love to have the preeminence"* more than all the doctrines of Christ and the apostles put together (3 Jn. 9-10). The plain truth is that men are called to *"live by every word that proceeds out of the mouth of God"* (Mt. 4.4; Acts 20.27). God's Word brings saints and true believers together, it does not scatter them (Jn. 10.16; 17.20-23; Eph. 1.10;4.11-16)! Hear the Lord, *". . . and they shall hear my voice; and there shall be one fold, and one shepherd!"*

God's laws and commandments are not to be trifled with, but rather reverenced. The Bible is not a smorgasbord or sumptuous buffet in which we can pick and choose whatever suits our personal likes and dislikes. This bespeaks of the essence of our church covenant in which we, according to the ordinance of God, have promised to "accept the Bible as the Word of God, to believe and practice its teachings rightly divided, with the New Testament as [our] rule of faith, practice, government, and discipline, and agree to walk together as one body in the light of the Gospel . . ." (Ex. 15.26; 19-5-8; Lev. 26.11-42; Deut. 6.1-9; 7.6-9; Jer. 7.23; Jn. 17.6, 8. 14; 1 Pet. 2.9; et al.).

To be sure, some teachings in the Bible are "weightier" and more important than others. Jesus made this clear (Mt. 23.23 see also 5.19); but still, all the teachings of Christ and the apostles are important and to be reverenced (Ps. 119.151; 2 Pet. 3.2; Jude 1.17). It is an outrageous presumption and great deception to assert, or even to leave the impression, that some of Jesus' and the apostles' teachings are not essential to Christian growth and the perfection of the body of Christ. For *"man does not live by bread alone but by every word that proceeds out of the mouth of God"* (Deut. 8.3; Mt. 4.4).

Again, though some teachings are weightier than others, all are to be kept sacred and to be observed (Jn. 17.6, 8, 14). We all should stand in awe of the Word of God, desiring the sincere milk and meat of the Word (Ps. 119.161; 1 Cor. 3.2; Heb. 5.12-14; 1 Pet. 2.2). The apostle said, *"I have not shunned to declare unto you all the counsel of God"* (Acts 20.27). The inspired psalmist emphasized that we should revere and keep *"all the judgments of [His] mouth"* (119.13); *"for all thy commandments are righteous"* (v. 172); and *"every one of thy righteous judgments endureth forever"* (v. 160). Accordingly, it is assumed everywhere in this psalm, as elsewhere in the Bible, that the plural expression of God's judgments, testimonies, statutes, precepts, commandments, ordinances, laws, words, and ways signify **"all"** of them.

In my fifty-two years of ministry, I have seen hundreds of ministers become shipwrecked by usurping the authority of God's Word and the church, supplanting it with personal/independent opinions and denominational traditions. I have had friends in the ministry become weak and superficial by the error mentioned above—"In essentials unity, in non-essentials liberty, in all things charity." Almost in every case, this philosophical formula has opened the door for liberalism and a license to sin. For if something is presumed to be non-essential then it tends to become non-important. We heard this very idea expressed by many in our former fellowship, and you know the result: it opened the door to compromise, superficiality, error, and worldliness.

Now observe, if some of the teachings of Jesus and the apostles are non-essential, who is to say what is essential and what is non-essential. Fundamentalists and most evangelicals believe that the essentials are the Virgin Birth, death and atoning sacrifice of Christ, His resurrection, and a few other core doctrines connected with these: the Trinity, observance of baptism, the Lord's Supper, etc. But under this idea, every half-baked minister, denomination, and independent church has historically watered down God's Word and opened the door for every ungodly practice—social drinking, abuse of tobacco and drugs, vulgar talk and profanity, body mutilation [piercing the ears, nose, lips, face, etc., and tattooing], various forms of fornication and sexual perversions, moral filth, and a worldly, fashionable Christianity. Such sacred institutions as marriage, the ordination of ministry, the infallibility of the Holy Scriptures, the doctrine and practice of footwashing, plainness in dress and our outward appearance, and even the doctrine of the church itself are disparaged and held in contempt. The biblical word holiness and all that it implies is seldom, if ever, mentioned. Carnal, lukewarm, and indifferent ministers and members naturally cater to the exaltation of their own opinions over against the church's authority and interpretation of the teachings of Christ and the apostles. The result is always confusion, chaos, and license [lawlessness] rather than Christian unity and edification; for it opens the way for every heresy and ungodly opinion and practice, all in the name of charity and liberty!

We readily acknowledge that doctrine in and of itself cannot transform lives and mold men into the image of Christ. That is the office and prerogative of the Holy Spirit. He inspired *"holy men of God"* to write the Bible (2 Sam. 3.2; Acts 1.16; 3.18; 2 Tim. 3.16; 2 Pet. 1.21), and He alone can quicken sinners to newness of life and sanctify believers (Jn. 3.5-8; Rom. 8.9-16; 2 Thess. 2.13; 1 Jn. 3.9; 5.18). But the Holy Spirit uses the Scriptures through ordained and anointed ministers and teachers to appeal to man's reason and inner spirit toward his salvation and transformation (1 Sam. 12.6-7; Is. 1.18; Jn. 5.39; Acts 17.2; 18.4, 19; 2 Tim. 3.15-17; et al).

Good doctrine informs and trains the conscience in the truths of God: and our corporate conscience [the church] bears witness to it in the

Holy Ghost (Jn. 1.9; Rom. 1. 19-20; 2.14-16; Gal. 4.6). As such, we can be guided by our conscience only if it is informed and trained by the Holy Scriptures (2 Tim. 3.15-17). The conscience is the judicial element in man's nature and makeup: it judges right and wrong, but it judges right and wrong on the basis of what it has been taught as right and wrong. This is the reason pagan mothers could offer up their babies to be burned and sacrificed to their pagan gods, for their consciences agreed with their twisted and perverted moral mindset. It has been said that you can follow your nose, but only if you get it pointed in the right direction to begin with; otherwise, it will lead you astray.

Certainly, it is more important to live a life of holiness than to know the doctrine of sanctification; but there would be little or no holiness in the lives of God's people if there was no doctrine of holiness. Like the law, Christian doctrine is a "schoolmaster" to bring us to Christ and the knowledge of His glorious Gospel (Gal. 3.24-25; 4.2-5; Rom. 7.7-13; 2 Tim 3.15-16; see also Ps. 119.33-48; et al).

Philosophers and liberal theologians have for years argued that the stars came before astrophysics and astronomy, and that flowers existed before botany, and that life existed before biology, and that God existed before theology. This is true: but without botany and biology, we would not know anything about the life and nature of plants and animals and their relationship to one another and their environment. Without these fields of knowledge, we would be left with old concepts that fostered witchcraft, pagan idolatries, and vain imaginations (Rom. 1.21-25; 2 Cor. 10.5). Without astronomy we would not know about the nature of the stars and how they work, and would be left with the superstitions and false concepts of astrology (horoscopes and worship of the stars); so also, without the Bible we would not know about the nature and character of God, His plan of salvation, His mysterious ways, and His kingdom and eternal purpose. We would forever be consigned to darkness under the impressions of false ideas hatched and entertained by sorcerers, philosophers, and false prophets.

Now observe, doctrine forms the skeleton of the body of Christ, the church. The vital organs of the body are held intact and given divine order by our skeletal system. The organs—heart, lungs, stomach, liver, gall bladder, etc.—would fall apart without the bone structure of the body. It is the same with the body of Christ (cf. Col. 2.19; Eph. 4.16; et al). Firm beliefs build strong character in believers; plain truths make for firm and settled convictions. Again, ["doctrinal beliefs in and of themselves are not a man's religion any more than the backbone is a man's personality; but without a healthy, straight backbone a man will be humpbacked and crippled"]. It is true with the whole skeletal system: the body would be weak and mushy without it and could not survive. Again, it is so with the body of Christ. A shallow-minded preacher once said, "Purity of heart and life are more important than correctness of doctrine." He was answered by a more sound-minded minister: "Healing is more important than the remedy; but without the remedy there would be no healing."

One final thing needs to be reiterated here; namely, that the church, in union and counsel with Christ and one another, is the final arbiter in matters of faith, doctrine, and discipline, in contrast to the individual minister and his private opinions (Mt. 16.17-19; 18.15-20; Acts 15.1-16.5; 1 Cor. 5.1-13; 1 Tim. 3.15). The church represents the corporate or collective conscience and mind of all the members in counsel together with God (Prov. 11.14; 15.22; 1 Cor. 2.16; 3.3-9; 12.12-31; Rom. 12.3-10; Eph. 4.1-16). Thus, the world-wide gathering of the church in General Assembly, not the individual person [overseer, pastor, or member] nor even the aggregate of local churches is *"the pillar and ground of the truth."* As such, the assembled body of the church in counsel with Christ and the elders is *"the highest tribunal of authority for the interpretation of Holy Scripture"* (cf. Acts 9.31; 15.1–16.5; 20.28; 1 Cor. 10.32; 11.22; 12.28; 1 Tim. 3.5, 15; et al).

In the divine system of decision-making, particularly regarding biblical interpretation and the establishment of doctrine, there is no place for individualism or local church autonomy and independence. Personal autonomy and independence are linked with the "works of the flesh"—namely, "strife," "divisions," "seditions," "heresies," "variance" [contentions, divisive arguments], etc. (1 Cor. 1.10-11; 11.16, 18-19; Gal. 5.20; 1 Tim. 3.5, 15; 2 Tim. 2.14-16; Titus 3.9-11; et al). An individual may indeed receive revelation from God through the Holy Spirit (Mt. 16.17-19; 2 Cor. 12.1-7; Acts 9.10-17; 15.12-19; Gal. 1.11-24; 2 Pet. 3.15-16): but the whole church in counsel [General Assembly] is ordained and commissioned to test whether that revelation is sound and consistent with the apostles' doctrine and fellowship (Acts 2.42; 15.1-19; 1 Cor. 14.26-33; Gal. 2.11; Eph. 2.20; 2 Pet. 1.16-21; 1 Jn. 4.1). After conferring together in General Assembly (Acts 15.1-28), the church hands down the *"decrees [dogmas] for to keep"* (16.4-5). Otherwise, the church will fall into chaos and confusion and end inevitably in denominationalism, independency, and apostasy.

Finally, it is of paramount importance to recognize a special ingredient in the establishment of doctrine and the decision-making process of the church; namely, that the participants in General Assembly be *"clothed with humility"* for the Assembly floor is a *"dreadful place!"* (Gen. 28.16-22; Mic. 6.8; Mt. 18.4; 23.11-12; Lk. 14.10-11; Acts 15. 22-28; Rom. 12.9-16; Eph. 4.1-3; Col. 3.12; Jas. 4.10; 1 Pet. 5.5-6; et al.). Zion Assembly is *"an habitation of God through the Spirit,"* seeking to be fully clothed with all the graces of the Spirit in expectation of fulfilling the apostle's vision of "a glorious church" (Eph. 2.19-22; 5.27). Only under the power of the Spirit's graces will we be able to *"walk by the same rule"* of faith; *"speak the same thing";* and *"be perfectly joined together in the same mind and in the same judgment"* (Rom. 15.1 Cor. 1.10; Phil. 3.16).

Section IV
"Simple Wedding Band"

The issue regarding married couples wearing a wedding band was settled in the organizational meeting conducted on April 18-20, 2004. After sufficient discussion, those present who had united with the church (85 courageous souls, seventeen of whom were ministers) agreed on our traditional stand against wearing gold, jewels, pearls, and costly attire, etc., excepting a simple wedding band. It was agreed that a plain wedding band was considered universally [both the church and in the world] to be nothing more or less than a cultural symbol of marriage, and not worn for gaudy and ostentatious reasons, nor to satisfy any sense of carnal pride. The point was made in fact that a simple wedding band rather strengthens our strict view of marriage as a sacred institution that is binding until the death of one of the partners. Only then is a marriage dissolved in the sight of God (Gen. 2.21-24; Mt. 5.31-32; 19.3-12; Mk. 10.2-12; 1 Cor. 7. 2-5, 10-11; Rom. 7.2-3).

This view, after a brief discussion, was endorsed unanimously by the General Assembly on September 24, 2004 (2004 *Assembly Minutes*, p. 22). A couple of questions lingered in the minds of a few brethren, but these were answered satisfactory for all concerned. Following that Assembly, the Presiding Bishop further explained the rationale behind the church's position. In a letter dated September 28, 2004, he noted regarding the wedding band: "The Assembly agreed with the report [of the Assembly Business Committee], particularly as it was enhanced by Pastor Ricky Graves' comment during the discussion, namely, that 'we all love and fellowship with each other regardless of the wedding band.' We have generally agreed since the April Conference in 2004 that our outward appearance in dress and behavior should be with simplicity and plainness, but a simple wedding band should be left to the discretion of each married couple.

Significantly, the few who had concerns did not oppose the wearing of a simple wedding band, but only wondered whether this line could be held without opening a floodgate for wearing all sorts of jewelry and encouraging a worldly and lavish lifestyle. The seventeen years since that time have proven this concern or fear to have been unfounded. The line has been held without any serious problems and without jeopardizing in the least bit our stand on plainness in dress and outward appearance. As already mentioned, it has rather reinforced our stand on the sacredness and indissolubility of a valid marriage. We do not apologize for our stand against the wearing of jewelry, showy adornments, and an intemperate, lavish lifestyle. For it is an apostolic teaching, and we are in these very last days committed to continuing in *"the apostles' doctrine and fellowship"* (Acts 2.42).

Our stand has served the church well; we have been able to hold to our traditional understanding and teaching against the wearing of gold, jewels, pearls, costly attire, and an extravagant lifestyle, without giving the appearance of being harsh, rigid, and narrow-minded. What we teach along this line is reasonable and scriptural, and, consequently, we have been able to support our position boldly and with conviction.

In support of our stand, we have the testimony of the Early Church Fathers—Clement of Rome, Ignatius, Justin Martyr, Irenaeus, Tertullian, Cyprian, Origen, Clement of Alexandria, Lactantius, and a host of others. They all lifted their pens and spoke with one voice against the folly of such extravagant practices, including the wearing of gold, pearls, precious stones [jewelry], costly attire, and a luxurious lifestyle. On a related subject, they also stood together against loud and gaudy cosmetics [for example, mascara and lipstick] which are in most cases designed to attract the attention of the opposite sex, which, in turn, has led in many cases to sexual seduction, adultery, fornication, and broken marriages. Let the admonitions and testimonies of Clement of Alexandria, Tertullian, Cyprian, Novatian, Commodianus, and Arnobius be sufficient here to prove the point.

Clement of Alexandria (c. 150-c. 215):

> "Love of dainties and love of wine, though great vices, are not of such magnitude as is fondness for finery . . . of gold, purple, and jewels . . . To such an extent, then, has luxury advanced, that not only is the female sex deranged about this frivolous pursuit, but men also are infected with the disease . . . The wearing of gold and the use of softer [luxurious] clothing is to be entirely prohibited. Irrational

impulses must be curbed . . . The Word prohibits us from doing violence to nature by boring the lobes of the ears . . . Let not their [women and babies] ears be pierced, contrary to nature in order to attach to them earrings."

Tertullian (c. 160-c. 225), a great second- and third century herald of holiness and Pentecostal power, wrote:

"Nowadays, women have every member of their bodies heavy laden with gold. [Was it] God who introduced the fashion of finely-cut wounds for the ears? Did he set so high a value upon the tormenting of His own work and the tortures of innocent infancy? For they learn to suffer with their earliest breath, in order that from those scars of the body . . . should hang I know not what."

Cyprian (d. 258):

"The characteristics of jewelry, garments, and the allurements of beauty are not fitting for anyone except prostitutes and immodest women."

Novatian (third century, d. c. 257):

"Why are the necks oppressed and hidden by outlandish stones? The prices of these without any workmanship— exceed the entire state of many persons."

Commodianus (third century, d. c. 240):

"Moreover, earrings hang down with very heavy weight! You bury your neck with necklaces! With gems and gold, you bind hands with an evil omen—hands that are worthy of God. Why should I speak of your dresses, or of the whole pomp of the devil? You reject the law when you wish to please the world."

Arnobius (d. c. 327). His ministry flourished in the late third- and early fourth century.

> "Did [the Lord] send souls so that, forgetting their importance and dignity as something divine, they would acquire gems, precious stones, and pearls—all at the expense of their purity? Did He send them to entwine their necks with such things, pierce the tips of their ears, and bind their foreheads with bands?"

It cannot be denied with impunity that these worldly practices have the tendency to say, "Hey look at me!" rather than point to the holiness of Christ and the glory of God (1 Cor. 1.29-31). This is the reason the Apostles and Early Church Fathers in their generations stood against such practices. Two prominent passages, one by the apostle Paul and one by the apostle Peter, seem sufficient here to establish the teaching of God's church.

> *"I will therefore that men pray everywhere, lifting up holy hands, without wrath and doubting. In like manner also, that women adorn themselves in modest apparel, with shamefacedness and sobriety; not with braided hair [plaited/elaborate showy hairstyles], or gold, or pearls, or costly array [dress]. But (which becometh women professing godliness) with good works"* (1 Tim. 2.7-10).

> *"Likewise, ye wives, be in subjection to your own husbands; that, if any obey not the word, they also may without the word be won by the chaste conversation [conduct/lifestyle] of the wives; While they behold your chaste conversation [conduct] coupled with fear [reverence]. Whose adorning let it not be that outward adorning of plaiting the hair [elaborate, showy hairdos], and of wearing gold, or of putting on apparel [costly, luxurious attire]; but let it be the hidden man of the heart, in that which is not corruptible, even the ornament of a meek and quiet spirit, which is in the sight of God of great price"* (1 Pet. 3.1-4).

The word *aidos* translated "shamefacedness" in 1 Tim. 2.9: *"lifting up holy hands* [in prayer and praise] . . . *with shamefacedness . . ."* indicates modesty, reverence, awe, godly fear. It is distinguished from the word *aischune* which is used elsewhere to signify "shame" or "disgrace," especially as one appears before the world, or in the sight of men who judge these transgressions as reproachful (Lk. 14.9; 2 Cor. 4.2; Phil. 3.19; Heb. 12.2; Jude 13; Rev. 3.18). Thus, rather than shamefacedness and reverence *aischune* carries the idea of haughtiness, shamefulness, and sometimes shamelessness.

Again, *aidos* signifies innate moral disgust and disdain for any dishonorable act, especially as the transgressor by introspection senses the reproach and guilt within himself for the act committed. The root of this word signifies "downcast eyes," in the sense of standing in awe before the Almighty God who sees all, knows all, and judges all. The publican in Lk. 18.10-14 thus *"would not lift up so much as his eyes to heaven"* in contrast to the haughty, shameless Pharisee. Significantly *aidos* ["modesty," "reverence," "godly fear"] is used only once again in Heb. 12.28: *"Wherefore . . . let us have grace, whereby we may serve God acceptably with reverence and godly fear."*

Now observe: there is in most cases a direct correlation between being shameless and haughty in one's dress and outward appearance, and, on the other hand, how one is on the inside, in the heart. This recalls the theological principle of *ad extra* and *ad intra*, which is a way of saying that however one acts on the outside indicates what he/she is like on the inside. The same is true with God himself since He works in a trinitarian manner on the outside, as Father, Son, and Holy Ghost [for example, God sent the Son and the Son sent the Holy Spirit, not vice-versa, that is, neither the Son nor the Holy Spirit sent the Father [Jn. 3.16; Lk. 24.49]. God must be therefore the same on the inside, that is, three persons in one Godhead grounded in the Father. The same is true with men. Haughty deeds indicate a haughty spirit and an inner disposition to defy the authority of God. This is the complaint of the Lord against *"the daughters of Zion"* in Is. 3.16-24. Their backslidden hearts were exposed in their arrogant spirit and worldly appearance. Like the harlot church in Rev. 17.1-6, they decked themselves with gold and all manner of precious jewels, fashionable attire, and flashy, expensive ornaments, being under the influence of the practices of the pagans and unregenerate world around them.

"Moreover the Lord saith, Because the daughters of Zion are haughty, and walk with stretched forth necks and wanton [deceiving/seductive] eyes, walking and mincing [dainty, prissy] as they go, and making a tinkling with their feet . . . In that day the Lord will take away the bravery [boastfulness, pride] of their tinkling ornaments . . . chains . . . bracelets . . . mufflers [jewel-studded ornaments] . . . earrings . . . rings . . . nose rings, jewels . . ." (vv. 16-22).

Plainly, the Lord does not want His people to "run with the crowd" or conform to the practices and traditions of the world around them (Ex. 23.2; Ezra 9.1-3; Rom. 12.2; 1 Pet. 1.14-16; 1 Jn. 2.15-16; et al.).

We will do well therefore, brethren, to follow Paul and Peter's inspired counsel in the texts cited, both of whom admonish us to dress and practice our faith with plainness, chastity, modesty, and simplicity, coupled with prayer, shamefacedness, sobriety, reverence, and godly fear to honor the presence of the Lord. Peter manifested this spirit of godly fear on several occasions. For example, in Jn. 21.7 when Jesus showed up on the shore and was recognized, John said, *"It is the Lord."* Upon hearing that, Peter immediately put on his fisher's coat and dove into the sea. The reference to him being "naked" signifies not absolute nakedness, but that he was improperly dressed, and, as such, unfit to be in the presence of the LORD. A similar meaning is to be understood in reference to the "nakedness" of King David (2 Sam. 6.14, 20). The meaning is that he humbled himself before the sovereign King of kings and Lord of lords. He laid aside his royal garments to honor the sovereign King of glory (see v. 6)! David, the king of Israel, stripped down to a linen ephod, rather than appearing in his royal robes, so that it would not seem he was competing with the King of glory.

So, it is important how we dress, especially when we assemble to worship and honor the LORD. In His presence, we should dress with dignity and with a certain formality, not in the common [vulgar] appearance of the world around us. What decent and God-fearing men and women would argue this point, for they would do as much in the presence of worldly dignitaries (see 2 Pet. 2.10; Jude 8). Except among profane and indecent people, if a couple were notified that the governor of their state was to honor their house with his/her presence at a certain time, would they not immediately see that both themselves and their children were properly dressed and well behaved for the special occasion? How much more then should we honor and reverence the LORD and His house!

But let us here return to the immediate subject at hand: the wearing of a simple wedding band. The wedding band, brethren, does not violate nor contradict our stand against a flashy and extravagant lifestyle, nor transgress against any of the scriptural and reasonable prohibitions against wearing of gold and jewelry for adornment listed in our *Abstract of Faith*. Rather it is simply a symbol of marital union and fidelity. It says, "I am married and committed to my wife or husband, and as such not available to anyone else." Further, its design symbolizes the holy wedlock and permanency of marriage, which is agreeable with our view of the indissolubility of marriage.

Brethren, let us be careful not to *"strain at a gnat, and swallow a camel"* (Mt. 23.24). This was Jesus' criticism of the scribes and Pharisees who magnified some less important teachings of the LORD at the expense of the *"weightier matters of the law"* (v. 23). To illustrate this point, earlier in the Assembly we launched a plan designed to stir up our zeal for outreach and evangelism by creating a lapel pin that symbolizes love and forgiveness and the graces of the Holy Spirit; and to help us bear in mind that the Lord desires for us to embody and manifest all these graces in the church. Now, just

97

as this pin is a symbol of something sacred and a way of opening the door for our Christian witness, so the simple wedding band is a symbol of something sacred and holy—namely, marriage, and may serve to open the door for us to explain and strengthen our view of marriage as a sacred and indissoluble union instituted by Christ. It seems inconsistent and unreasonable to accept this simple 7x70 pin and yet oppose the wearing of a simple wedding band. What we are opposed to, brethren, is childish, if not foolish, ornamentation and a luxurious lifestyle, both of which throw our precious resources to the wind and feed pride and a carnal appetite.

In the final analysis, however, brethren, we neither encourage nor prohibit the wearing of a simple wedding band, but rather leave it up to the discretion of each couple who are properly married in the eyes of God and the church. Let us therefore consider this to be the settled opinion of the General Assembly and our churches everywhere.

Section V
"Financing the Expansion and Development of Our International Ministries Complex"

Those who have gathered here this week are eyewitnesses to the working of the hand of God in the construction of this marvelous International Ministries Complex. The original building was an IGA supermarket [built over 50 years ago] that later became an old greasy "chop shop" of junk cars. We purchased the building in November 2003, anticipating the restoration of the church in the imminent future, which happened only a few months later on April 20, 2004. Our faithful ministers and members have since then been *"laborers together with God"* in the on-going development and construction of this beautiful and adequate multi-complex. Your prayers, hands-on labor, and faithful giving have made this possible by the grace of God. (Let's give the Lord and each other a handclap of praise).

In 2009 mention was made of needing additional space to facilitate our International Staff and international events, particularly the

School of Ministry, General Assemblies, and day to day operations in the offices. In 2011 we inaugurated "The Prophets' Plan" to raise funds to expand our Headquarters operations and to make our vision of a Bible College become a reality. The Prophets' Plan is based on the plan launched by Elisha to build a larger building to house "the sons of the prophets" recorded in 1 Kg. 6.1-5. In this plan each one of the prophets cut down a tree, hewed it out, and fit it in the new building. To mimic what they did, we estimated the cost of a tree including hewing it out and fitting it in place in our building. The estimation in modern currency was about $800. Our ministers and members responded generously and enthusiastically, and we raised in one year almost $90,000. Many gave an amount equal for two trees and some three and some as many as ten. The next year our people again responded well and gave about $70,000. With this money we took out a loan at the bank, and completely renovated the old IGA supermarket to facilitate the beginnings of our International Ministries Complex.

The next year (2013) there were stirrings among us to build an Assembly Tabernacle. The aim was to restore not only the spirit, doctrine, and fellowship of the church, but to build again ministries and facilities that had been abandoned in our former fellowship; including the Assembly Tabernacle and the closing of Tomlinson College, both of which were grievously and reproachfully shut down or destroyed in the early 1990s. These things signaled to the "other sheep" and to the world at large that we were a dying church. We were going backward, not forward.

One aspect of the Restoration was therefore to build an Assembly Tabernacle so that we would not have to depend on others for a place to have our General Assemblies and to avoid the continual rise in costs to rent facilities. But also, we wanted the comforts and conveniences of "home," that is, we wanted to worship as early and as late as we wished and to have the right to turn our lights on and off as we wished, without being under the thumb and restrictions imposed on us by the owners of the facilities from whom we were renting.

One more thing added to the equation of building an Assembly Tabernacle: it was generally taken for granted that our International Ministries Complex would not be complete without an Assembly Tabernacle. Accordingly, the Presiding Bishop recommended in the 11th Annual Assembly held in Knoxville in 2014 a financial plan to build a Tabernacle. It was called The King's Plan because King Joash desired to repair the House of God during his illustrative reign, which had been broken up by the sons of the wicked Athaliah, the daughter of Jezebel. An excerpt from the annual address explains the plan.

"Now in order to build a Tabernacle, I am proposing that we receive an offering on a regular basis to finance this vision, using for a pattern Moses' plan in Exodus 30.12-16 to build the Tabernacle in the Wilderness, which King Joash modified to repair the House of God in his day (see 2 Kings 12 and 2 Chronicles 24). To give "day by day" and "year to year" toward this fund (according to Joash's plan), we simply need to incorporate it as part of the church's regular financial system. The pastor or duly appointed Tabernacle booster could promote and receive once a month a Tabernacle Fund offering. We could design and make offering boxes to be displayed by the local churches in conspicuous places, and on the boxes write the inscription, "Tabernacle Fund—Let Us Rise Up and Build" or "There shall be a Tabernacle" (an allusion to Isaiah 4.6), or something to that effect. Then as the funds come in each month, the money can be counted by the local treasurer and sent to Headquarters with the regular monthly report . . . If this plan meets with the approval of the Assembly Business Committee, the committee can draw up a resolution to present to the Assembly for consideration and approval."

The ABC enthusiastically presented the plan to the General Assembly during the business session that afternoon and the Assembly adopted it unanimously. We were thus off and running zealously with the vision for a new Assembly Tabernacle.

But then certain things transpired that interrupted our immediate plans.

First, the owner of the property that joined our property on the East side of our building suddenly decided to sell us his property in January 2016. After some negotiating [haggling] he agreed to sell it to us for $160,000. We then called a special Minister's Council, virtually a special-called General Assembly (the first one in our history), and the Assembly agreed unanimously to put on hold our immediate plans to build a tabernacle to purchase this property: for we didn't want to pass up the opportunity (see Annual Address in 13th Annual Assembly Minutes, 2016, pp. 97-100). The Lord helped us, and we wondrously paid off the indebtedness for this property and our earlier bank note on the original property in less than two years.

Second, we then agreed to build a two-story 10,000 sq. ft. wing onto our existing property to add much needed office and storage space for our International Office operations, and to house our envisioned Bible College and also provide better facilities for our School of Ministry Institute. This was the fulfillment of a vision cast in 2011.

Third, we decided then (15th Annual Assembly, 2018), to consolidate our Tabernacle Fund, Bible College Fund, and the existing construction loan, and all future construction loans into "one simple building fund account" and call it the "International Properties Building Fund" [IPBF]. (See Presiding Bishop's Annual Address, pp. 66-68 and the ABC report, pp. 46-47). This resolution too was accepted unanimously by the Assembly.

Joining together The Prophet's Plan and The King's Plan into the IPBF has worked marvelously for us. God has honored it because it is based on His own desire which He put in the heart of Moses, Elisha, the sons of the prophets, King David, King Solomon, and King Joash in their desire to build and repair God's House. Now then, brethren, let's pick up where we left off, turning our attention again to building an Assembly Tabernacle. To do so, we will have to work on two fronts: paying off our current loan which financed the new wing of our International Ministries Complex and at the same time raising funds for the envisioned Assembly Tabernacle. The Good News is we don't need another financial plan. We have it! namely, The Prophet's Plan and The King's Plan which we have merged together into what we have designated as the IPBF: for this has proven to be a sufficient and inspirational financial strategy, one which God Himself has inspired, and one which Moses, Elisha, the sons of the prophets, and King David, King Solomon, and King Joash [called King Jehoash elsewhere] implemented during their respective reigns. We just need to implement this God-ordained strategy willingly and cheerfully.

The IPBF has three important financial sources.

1) The church ruled in the 15th Annual Assembly in 2018 that since our Bible College will be the most formidable and utilized facility for teaching and training and sending forth of laborers to the mission fields, twenty percent [20%] of the funds received for World Missions is to be put into the IPBF toward financing the expansion of the International Ministries Complex" (note 15th Annual Assembly Minutes, pp. 46-47).

2) A monthly offering is to be received in the local churches and sent to the General Treasurer with the regular monthly report (see 15th Annual Assembly Minutes, 2018, p. 47).

3) Each year ["from year to year"] according to the example of The King's Plan in 2 Chron. 24.5-14, note esp. v. 5 we receive a big jubilee offering toward this end—to build God's house and keep
it repaired.

Finally, brethren, let it always be borne in mind in preparing to build an Assembly Tabernacle that

> "[We need to] get in the spirit of it, like the sons of the prophets did in Elisha's day, and the people of God in Moses' day, and all of Israel did in King David and King Solomon's days, and in King Joash's day. There is nothing that we cannot accomplish together if we get in the spirit of it. That's how the magnificent temple of God was built on Mount Zion [and kept repaired]. The House of God [the Temple] was first in David's heart, and the vision and affection for it then took hold of the people of God. The spirit of giving got into David and then all the leaders and the people, and they gave in today's currency more than two trillion dollars ($2,000,000,000,000) in gold, silver, precious stones, brass, iron, marble, and precious woods to build a house worthy of the true and living God! The account is given in 1 Chron. 29. The key to it all is shown in vv. 2–14, namely, they caught a vision of God's house, and the vision conditioned their affections and will to make it a reality. David said, '*I have prepared with all my might for the house of my God*' (v. 2); and the people then '*offered willingly . . . and gave . . . to the treasure of the house of the Lord*' (vv. 6-8). And when all was given, '*Then the people rejoiced, for that they offered willingly . . . with a perfect heart to the LORD: and David the king also rejoiced with great joy*' (v. 9). And when Solomon built the house of God there was nothing like it in all the earth!"

Section VI
"Suffering: A Mark of the Church"

As the church gradually *"departed from the faith"* in the early centuries of Christianity [beginning not long after the Apostles past off the scene of action], the children of God were scattered abroad by false teachings, heresies, pagan influences, and hateful divisions, with each schismatic group claiming to be the "true church."

[Note: This apostasy was plainly seen and foretold by Jesus and the apostles: see Acts 20.29–31; 1 Tim. 4.1–3; 2 Tim. 3.1–8, 13; 2 Pet. 2.1-3, 10–22; 3.2–17; Jude 3–4, 6–16; Rev. 2.5–22; see also Jesus' warning in Mt. 7.13–20; et al. The great apostasy as well as the restoration of the church was also predicted by the prophets in the Old Testament and demonstrated by types and shadows in the church in the wilderness, the church under the old covenant (Acts 7.38). See Is. 2.2-3; 25.5–6; 49.1–6; 52.1–10; 54.1–10; 60.1-14; Jer. 2.1–4.31; Ezek. 16.2–63; 37.1–28; et al.]

The identity and distinctiveness of the true church was, accordingly, gradually lost in the confusion and apostasy. This prompted the largest faction of the disruption—the Roman Catholic Church [RCC] to develop what came to be known as the "marks of the church" or "notes of the church." These marks were as follows: **"one"** [meaning one visible, united body], **"holy"** [meaning set apart by the Lord], **"catholic"** [meaning universal in its government and teachings], and **"apostolic"** [meaning her leaders (bishops)] were the duly appointed successors to the apostles. These four marks were accepted by the Council of Nicea in AD 325 and incorporated as part of the Nicene Creed. It was a way for the RCC to represent herself as being the "true church" and to distinguish herself from all the "heretical" and "schismatic" groups. The RCC thereafter claimed to be exclusively the "one," "holy," "catholic," and "apostolic" church.

Our response to this claim by the RCC is what Voltaire said regarding the Holy Roman Empire, that it was neither Holy nor Roman nor an Empire; so too, the RCC is neither One nor Holy nor Catholic nor Apostolic. Ironically, by the adoption of these four marks, the Roman Church had indicted and incriminated herself, for they proved in fact that the RCC was not God's true church.

During the Protestant Reformation beginning in the sixteenth century, the mainline reformers and denominations stressed only two marks: namely, right preaching of the Word of God [meaning right doctrine] and right administration of the sacraments. Like the RCC, the mainline reformers [Lutherans, Calvinists, etc.] indicted themselves: they did not measure up to these two marks, and in fact, held to many of the old errors of Roman Catholicism and developed new errors, including "forensic justification," "positional holiness," the creation of the denominational system and the invention of the "invisible church" myth.

None of these views held by Roman Catholics, Anglicans [Episcopalians], Orthodox churches, and Protestants are sufficient or satisfactory to identify God's church, and some are "damnable heresies" and completely deceiving. We agree in Zion Assembly that the church is **one** [in covenant union and walking together as a *"peculiar people"* under the same rule of faith and government [Ex. 19-5-8; 1 Pet. 2.9; 1 Cor. 1.10; Phil. 3.16]; **holy** [meaning not just *"set apart"* but actually *"made righteous"* in Christ through the sanctifying and transforming power of the Holy Spirit and by practicing holiness as a way of life [Jn. 3.3-8; Rom. 5.19; 6.1-7, 17-22; 8.1, 9-13; Eph. 5.26-27; Col. 1.13; 1 Pet. 1.22-23. The holiness of God's church also extends to its inner self-discipline as a covenant body, in which the government of the church readily uses disciplinary measures to counsel, reprove, and where necessary, exclude disorderly and unruly members [Mt. 18.17-20; Jn. 20.23; 1 Cor. 5.1-13]; **catholic** or "universal," that is, its unity in faith, doctrine, and government extends to wherever there are Zion Assembly churches and members throughout the world [Acts 15.1–16.5; 1 Cor. 4.17; 7.17; 2 Cor. 11.28; Jas. 1.1; 1 Pet. 1.1–2; Phil. 3.16]; **apostolic**, that is, Zion Assembly is continuing faithfully in the apostles' doctrine and fellowship [Acts 1.13-14; 2.42; Eph. 2.20; 2 Pet. 3.2, 15-16]. The object of its elders and ministers is *"to present every man perfect in Christ Jesus"* (Col. 1.28), and to *"make ready"* a chaste bride to be presented to Christ *"without spot, or wrinkle, or any such thing; but that it be holy and without blemish"* (2 Cor. 11.2-3; Eph. 4.11-16; 5.26–27; Rev. 19.7-8).

To accomplish the monumental task that has been handed down to us, we can identify in large measure with many of the fundamentals of the "radical reformers" of the Great Reformation [Anabaptists, Huguenots, Moravians, Quakers, Mennonites, Brethren, Dunkers, etc.] in the sixteenth- and seventeenth centuries; for they identified the church as a visible, interdisciplinary body, seeking to teach, counsel, and discipline its converts in biblical faith and truth until the image of Christ was stamped on every member.

Following in this vein of thinking, Zion Assembly has concluded that the marks of the church are not merely the four marks mentioned in the Nicene Creed, but include the same marks that identify the moral attributes of Christ. In other words, the church under the metaphor of the body of Christ is the embodiment and express image of Christ's nature and characteristics—love, joy, peace, holiness, justice, judgment, righteousness, kindness, tenderness, humility, etc. He dwells in His church and shines His glory and holiness out through her as a witness to the world! She incorporates His life into hers and is thus identified as His body and His bride (Mt. 16.24-26; Jn. 17.1-21; 2 Cor. 3.2-3; Phil. 2.5-8; 1 Pet. 2.21-24; 1 Jn. 2.6; et al).

The radical reformers also identified "suffering" as a mark of the true church. This is a mark that is often ignored, dismissed, and in many instances vehemently contradicted by contemporary preachers, common denominations, independent churches and especially by maverick televangelists and "health and wealth" preachers. Yet this teaching is boldly set forth in the teachings of Christ and the apostles and was glaringly demonstrated in their lives and martyrdoms.

The Anabaptists suffered almost as much from the hands of the Protestant Reformers as they did from Roman Catholics. Millions of Anabaptists suffered unspeakable persecution, not only physical violence and martyrdom, but verbal assaults—slander, malicious gossip, false accusations, hate speech, and various forms of deprivation, discomforts, and humiliation. It included also being shunned, ostracized, and marginalized by the common churches. This is the reason our forefathers and foremothers in Zion Assembly identified themselves with the Anabaptists.

But they also saw suffering exemplified by Christ and the apostles in the Scriptures, and by sincere believers in the second- and third centuries and throughout the Dark Ages. Jesus Himself is our primary and perfect example of suffering, which we will notice more closely in a moment. But first it is important to see how the prophets envisioned Him and typified His suffering in the Old Testament. A passage in Psalm 42 drives home the point.

"Deep calleth unto Deep"

"As a hart panteth after the water brooks, so panteth my soul after there, O God. My soul thirsteth for God, for the living God: when shall I come and appear before God? My tears have been my meat [bread] day and night, while they continually say unto me, where is thy God? When I remember these things, I pour out my soul in me: for I had gone with the multitude, I went with them to the house of God, with the voice of joy and praise, with a multitude that kept holyday. Why art thou cast down, O my soul? and why art thou disquieted in me? hope thou in God: for I shall yet praise him for the help of his countenance. O my God, my soul is cast down within me: therefore will I remember thee from the land of Jordan, and of the Hermonites, from the hill Mizar. Deep calleth unto deep at the noise of thy waterspouts: all thy waves and thy billows are gone over me. Yet the LORD will command his lovingkindness in the daytime, and in the night his song shall be with me, and my prayer unto the God of my life. I will say unto God my rock, Why hast thou forgotten me? why go I mourning because of the oppression of the enemy? As with a sword in my bones, mine enemies reproach me; while they say daily unto me, Where is thy God? Why art thou cast down, O my soul? and why art thou disquieted within me? hope thou in God: for I shall yet praise him, who is the health of my countenance, and my God" (Ps. 42.1-11).

This psalm has a primary reference to the anguish and sufferings of David during his lifetime, especially during the grief and hardships suffered under King Saul who was envious of him, hated him bitterly, and sought to have him assassinated. But it seems this psalm more fittingly describes David during the betrayal and revolt of his vain and ungodly son, Absalom. During Absalom's revolt, David was exiled from his throne in Zion, deprived of worshipping in the Temple [a tent that at that time housed the Ark of the Covenant], and left wandering along the Jordan River and up in the mountain region of Mount Hermon more than a hundred miles northeast of Jerusalem. The headwaters of the Jordan River proceeded for the most part from this mountainous region which served the psalmist to express by analogy and metaphor his anguish, spiritual suffering, and feeling of isolation from God and the people of God. Here David reflected on his pathetic state and narrated the anguish of his soul and his strained and seemingly broken relationship with God, who is referred to here and elsewhere in the Hebrew as Elohim [*"the Almighty God"*] instead of *Yahweh/Jehovah*, the covenant God of salvation who descends to redeem and sanctify His people. Significantly, however, in the one instance that the name *Yahweh/Jehovah* is used (v. 8), we are most encouraged and illuminated; for, despite the overwhelming struggles that David was facing, he says, *"Yet the LORD [Jehovah] will command His lovingkindness in the daytime, and in the night His song shall be with me, and my prayer unto the God of my life."*

As a prefiguration of Christ and His sufferings, David was betrayed by his friends, hunted by his enemies, taunted by pagan unbelievers as well as by his own brethren in Israel. They *"say daily unto me, Where is thy God?"* (vv. 3, 10). Some of his own people had betrayed him and mocked him, for it seemed to them that because David was exiled from the house of God, he was cast out altogether. But see, just because you are unjustly forced out of God's house does not mean you have lost your God (cf. 3 Jn. 9-10). See it doesn't follow that just because our enemies may rob us of our buildings and Bibles that they have also robbed us of our God. King Solomon would acknowledge this in his dedicatory prayer for the glorious temple on Mount Zion. He said, we all know You are greater and more magnificent that anything or anyone under heaven, and that the *"heaven of heavens cannot contain Thee: how much less this house which I have built!"* (2 Chron. 6.17). He thus anticipated the Gospel age when God would dwell in the hearts of men.

During his exile, David communed with God in Jordan and in the mountains of Hermon north of Jerusalem; for His presence was not bound to representative symbols—arks and banners and temples made with hands, or prayer shawls or rams' horns, and the sacrifices of goats and bulls. David's trials and troubles only served to *"awaken"* him to that truth and reality, and to His need to talk with God on mount Mizar, located in the chain of the Hermonite mountain range. Even then David knew that God dwells within His people and could not be contained in a tent or ark. When he was kicked out of office and the house of God unjustly, He took God with him! His enemies were left with the old apostate tent; whereas David went forward with God and a prophetic vision to build the magnificent temple of God on Mount Zion.

David was tempted, tried, had stumbled, and was chastised by the Lord. But behold, he was made perfect through suffering: his hardships and feeling of isolation and betrayals gave occasion for him to call upon God with unflinching faith and deep passion, pleading for the Lord to intercede for him. God in turn honored and rewarded his faith by pouring out His gracious favors and restoring him to his throne in Jerusalem. But more importantly the great trial restored David's relationship with God: for because of his own faults and backsliding (Ps. 51.1-19), it was first necessary for a holy God to pull back from him, to chastise him, and deprive him of intimacy with Him. More than anything else David longed for soul-intimacy with God as a thirsty deer [gazelle] pants [cries out] for water. He said, *"My soul thirsteth after God, for the living God"* (Ps. 42.1), a thirst in his soul that only God Himself could quench. Now observe: David uses thirst instead of hunger to describe his anguish, for it denotes a more desperate situation, in that a man can live longer without food than water, that is, the lack of water makes one more desperate! His tears were his meat—he lived on them, was strengthened by them, and his soul was seasoned by the salt of them, and perhaps his natural meat also.

Under the pain of this great trial, David desired to be in the House of God, worshipping and fellowshipping with the people of God; observing the divine ordinances instituted by the Lord through the leadership of Moses in ancient days (v. 4). He recalls the voice of singing, praise, and shouts of rejoicing in the House of God and longs to hear and see them again (Ps. 48.1; 132.9, 16; see also 137.3; 142. 2-5; 147.12). His love and admiration for God's House is everywhere noticed in David's writings and prophecies. Zion is exalted as the center for God's salvation, righteousness, justice, authority, and wisdom (Ps. 48.11-14; 51.16-19; 102.16; 132.11-18; see also Is. 2.2-4; 33.20). *"Beautiful for situation, the joy of the whole earth is Mount Zion"* (48.2); *"Glorious things are spoken of thee, O City of God!"* (Ps. 87.3); *"Walk about Zion . . . tell the towers thereof. Mark ye well her bulwarks, consider her palaces; that ye may tell it to the generations following"* (48.12-13). *"The Lord loveth the gates of Zion more than all the tents [dwellings] of Jacob"* (87.2). When the Ark of the Covenant was in the hands of the Philistines and afterward lost in the fields of *Kiriathjearim,* he made a promise that he would not enter his house nor go up into his bed, nor give sleep to his eyes or slumber to his eyelids until he found it and brought it to Mount Zion, so that it could be enclosed with a tent and established as the center of worship and adoration for God's people (Ps. 132.1-6). He longed to see and feel again the presence of the Living God in the midst of the church (Ps. 42. 2).

Much of David's spiritual agony, here and elsewhere, came as He remembered being in right standing with the Lord and being together with the saints of God in the house of God, worshipping and rejoicing together with them on the sabbath days. It was thus that, under divine chastisement, his soul was disquieted [troubled, distressed, disturbed] within him; yet he knew by his past experiences that the LORD of the covenant pours out mercy and kindnesses in forgiveness and reconciliation. David is a perfect example that one cannot fall so low that God cannot reach down and pick him up, for the Lord will always keep covenant with the seed of David, that is, Christ and His seed—those born of God by the incorruptible Word of God (Gal. 3.16, 29; 1 Pet. 1.22–23; 2.2; Jn. 1.13; 1 Jn. 3.9; 4.7; 5.1, 4, 18). Listen to the prophet:

> *"My mercy will I keep for him [David/Christ] forevermore, and my covenant shall stand fast with him. His seed also will I make to endure forever, and his throne as the days of heaven. If his children forsake my law and walk not in my judgments; If they break my statutes and keep not my commandments; then will I visit their transgressions with the rod, and their iniquity with stripes. Nevertheless, my lovingkindness will I not utterly take from him, nor suffer my faithfulness to fail. My covenant will I not break, nor alter the thing that is gone out of my lips. Once I sware by my holiness that I will not lie unto David [Christ]. His seed shall endure forever, and His throne as the sun before me. It shall be established forever as the moon, and a faithful witness in heaven. Selah"* (Ps. 89.28-37; see also 132.12; Mt.10.22; Heb. 3.6; Col. 1.23).

The saying in Ps. 42.7 that *"Deep calleth unto deep,"* many commentators believe to mean a tornadic-type funnel of water producing one wave after another, destroying everything in its path; and that David used this metaphor here to describe the troubles and afflictions that had overwhelmed him. Notwithstanding, even if there is an allusion here in this sense, it seems more fittingly that it depicts the depths of God Himself—Father, Son, and Holy Spirit— calling to the depths of David's soul, pleading for him to return to Him with all his heart and soul! Pleading with him to awake to righteousness; urging him to gird up the loins of his mind and trust in the power and goodness of God. Though it could mean the noise of tornadic funnels and a tsunami of waves beating against him, yet God is greater in power and deliverance.

Two phrases stand out in this Psalm: *"My God"* and *"My soul."* It reminds us of Solomon's cry for the Shulamite woman [a type of the church-bride], who had wandered off after their betrothal, typifying the depths of God crying out for His wandering covenant people to return to Him, saying, *"Return, return, O Shulamite; return, return, that we may look upon thee . . ."* (Song 7.13). At the same time, it may mean the depths of David crying out to the depths of God, pleading for forgiveness and crying out for reconciliation, trusting ultimately in God's lovingkindness. He acknowledges that the Almighty is his *"rock"* and *"the health of [his] countenance,"* and as such, he still *"[hopes] in God . . . and shall yet praise Him"* (v. 11).

Though God had disquieted [troubled, distressed, disturbed] David's soul; yet the "sweet psalmist" says, *"the Lord will command his lovingkindness in the daytime, and in the night his song shall be with me, and my prayer unto the God of my life"* (v. 8). By inward reflection and a deep personal dialogue within himself, as if his soul is speaking with his natural reason, he thus reproves himself, saying, *"Why go I mourning because of the oppression of the enemy? . . . Why art thou cast down, O my soul?"* We learn from this example that faith brings the victory (1 Jn. 5.4)! A soul that is cast down can yet *"hope in God"* and *"praise Him"* and win the victory against any foe.

This is the Gospel of Christ and His Kingdom and the nature of our Christian pilgrimage on earth, in which, accordingly, even the most saintly among God's people sometimes drift away and suffer separation from Him: for God's holiness requires Him not only to back off from sinfulness and disobedience (*"But your iniquities have separated between you and your God, and your sins have hid His face from you, that He will not hear"* (Is. 59.2; Hos. 5.6; Prov. 1.24-30), but also from lukewarmness, indifference, and lack of intimacy with God. *"So then, because thou art lukewarm, and not hot or cold, I will spew [vomit] thee out of my mouth"* (Rev. 3.14). *"Stir up the gift that is in you"* (2 Tim. 1.6). *"Awake to righteousness and sin not"* (1 Cor. 15.34). *"Awake thou that sleepest . . . and Christ shall give thee light"* (Eph. 5.14; Rom. 13.11).

See, if our faith is worth anything, it is worth everything (Mk. 8.34-38). There is no room for neutrality or indifference! God desires that we have a *"vehement zeal"* to live and work for Him (Song 8.6; Mt. 3.10-12; Col. 3.1-3). All of us should follow the example of Christ, of whom it was said, *"The zeal of thine house hath eaten me up."* Abraham [Sarah], Isaac [Rebecca], Jacob, [Rachel], Boaz [Ruth] Samson, Elijah, David, Peter, James and John and others, all great men and women of God stumbled during their lifetimes. But those who have had a deep and intimate relationship with the Lord cannot remain in that state without either repenting and returning to a justified and blameless state with the Lord or else backsliding and becoming more callous, often to the point of reprobation.

In fact, God allows us to drift away and to be found wanting so that we might more appreciate His joy and victory. He lets us dry-up and experience severe thirst to make us appreciate the Fountain of Life and drink more deeply from the "Rivers of Living Water"; He withholds mercy so that we might learn to respect and appreciate His mercifulness; He takes away our peace and joy so that we might feel the impact of our sadness and emptiness without Him.

"Cheer up my brother, we'll sing in the sunshine."

Life cannot be all sunshine. An old proverb says, "All sunshine makes a desert." There must be times of darkness to make us appreciate the light; of thirst to appreciate water; of reproof to appreciate mercy; of chastisement to appreciate forgiveness and lovingkindness; of affliction to appreciate our health. For in this present age *"the whole creation groaneth and travaileth in pain together until now"* (Rom. 8.22). And the *"whole creation"* includes the church and all the living saints, and, indeed, especially the church until she reaches her final glorious state in the heavenly bliss of God's eternal Kingdom (vv. 18-30).

In another place the apostle says, *"[We] are changed in the same image [the glory of the Lord] from glory to glory, even as by the*

Spirit of the Lord" (2 Cor. 3.18). And still in another place this same apostle says that our perfection will continue to unfold, *"Till we all come in the unity of the faith, and of the knowledge of the Son of God, unto a perfect man, unto the measure of the stature of the fulness of Christ"* (Eph. 4.13-16); the meaning of which, it seems to me, is that in our walk with God [both individually and corporately as the body of Christ] we will have an ever-increasing amount of His grace and illuminating power until we reach the glory of His heavenly Kingdom (Rom. 8.23-30; 2 Pet. 1.11).

But now observe, in between the times of glory in this present age, there must be trials, tribulations, hardships, afflictions, and struggles. Only in this way can we go from glory to glory! For the deeper revelation of God is obtained only through chastisement and suffering and makes our way forward ever brighter and more glorious—step by step, one glory to another: until we are all fully glorified together and *"caught up"* to meet Jesus in the air (Eph. 1.10; 1 Thess. 4.17-19; 1 Cor. 15.53-55).

David a Type of Christ

More importantly Psalm 42 looks forward to the sufferings of Christ, beginning with His rejection by His own people to His atoning sacrifice, resurrection, exaltation, and glorification. David's life and kingship was a prefiguration of Christ's, which included Jesus' anguish, afflictions, hardships, and rejection. And it serves also as a pattern for the church to emulate; a pattern that will ultimately be fulfilled in a perfect, triumphant church *"without spot, or wrinkle, or any such thing"* (Eph. 5.27).

The key ingredient is suffering! The human Jesus was made perfect through suffering (Heb. 2.10), that is, it was necessary for Him to qualify Himself to be the *"captain of our salvation."* Having become a man in the Incarnation, He afterward sanctified Himself and endured temptations and ultimately died by way of crucifixion to become our *"merciful and faithful High Priest"* (Jn. 17.17; Heb. 10.11-

17). Having triumphed over every foe, He is now able to *"make propitiation [for sinners]"* and to mediate and advocate for His church and for all saints everywhere (1 Jn. 2.1). *"For in that He Himself hath suffered being tempted, He is able to succor [aid/help] them who are tempted"* (v. 18).

Our Suffering Savior

"Looking unto Jesus the author and finisher of our faith; who for the joy that was set before Him endured the cross, despising the shame, and is set down on the right hand of the throne of God. For consider Him that endured such contradiction of sinners against Himself, lest ye be wearied and faint in your minds. Ye have not yet resisted unto blood, striving against sin. And ye have forgotten the exhortation which speaketh unto you as unto children, My son, despise not thou the chastening of the Lord, nor faint when thou are rebuked of Him: for whom the Lord loveth He chasteneth, and scourgeth every son whom He receiveth. If ye endure chastening, God dealeth with you as with sons; for what son is he whom the farther chasteneth not? But if ye are without chastisement, whereof we are all partakers, then are ye bastards and not sons. Furthermore we have had fathers of our flesh which corrected us, and we gave them reverence: shall we not much rather be in subjection unto the Father of spirits, and live? For they verily for a few days chastened us after their own pleasure; but he for our profit, that we might be partakers of His holiness. Now no chastening for the present seemeth to be joyous, but grievous: nevertheless afterward it yieldeth the peaceable fruit of righteousness unto them which are exercised thereby" (Heb. 12.2-11).

"This day hath I begotten Thee"

Now observe: Jesus was God's Son when He was supernaturally incarnated (this we all know and celebrate every Christmas—Lk. 1.26-38), but He became God's Son in a peculiar way when He fulfilled His appointed role as a man: to be crucified and to die upon the Cross! For that, for His faithfulness even unto death, He was exalted to sit with His Father in His throne in glory and to rule and reign over the earth and the whole cosmic creation (Ps. 2.7; Phil. 2.5-9; Heb. 1.5; 5.5). His obedience unto death won Him a special status and new relationship with the eternal Father; of which His resurrection, transfiguration and glorification was the seal, in contrast to His birth in Bethlehem (Ps. 89.25-29; 2 Sam. 7.4-17; Acts 13.32-39; 1 Cor. 15.24-30; Phil. 2.5-10; Heb. 1.5-9; 5.5-9). He is now the Anointed One and has received the eternal Kingdom and has been exalted to His eternal position as King of kings and Lord of lords.

"Consider Christ Jesus"

Jesus was physically beaten, bruised, and smitten. Jagged nails were driven through His feet and hands; a Roman soldier's sword pierced His side; and a crown of thorns was driven into His skull. These cruel measures caused *"His visage [appearance] [to be] marred [disfigured] more than any man"* (Is. 52.14; 53.3-12). The innocent Lamb suffered immeasurable pain and suffering in His body. But more than the physical agony inflicted upon His broken body, He suffered mentally, psychologically, and spiritually. He was betrayed and abandoned by His friends and His church [that is, Israel under the Old Covenant] (Jn. 1.11). He was rejected, grieved, and stricken.

There is a liturgical poem written during the Middle Ages called "O Happy Fault" or "O Blessed Sin." It probes deep into the mystery of Adam's sin that plunged the whole race of man into sin and separation from God. Yet if Adam had not fallen, we would have never known the depths of God's love in and through Christ! God did not ordain or decree Adam to sin, but His omniscience saw that he would, and thus, accordingly, our loving and wonderful God prepared the remedy: man's redemption through the sacrifice of His only begotten Son (Rev. 13.8).

Jesus endured one disappointment after another yet remained faithful to His heavenly Father. Judas Iscariot betrayed Him; Peter at one point turned away and denied Him; indeed, many of His followers walked away from Him when He talked about suffering and having to be killed and crucified (Mt. 16.21-23; Jn. 6.60-66). *"He came to His own and His own received Him not."* He was *"wounded in the house of [His] friends"* (Zech. 13.6). His brethren after the flesh hated Him and cried out during His trial, *"Crucify Him, crucify Him!"* Their fathers had persecuted and killed the prophets and now schemed a way to have the Heir of the eternal kingdom killed (Mt. 21.33-43; Lk. 11.47-50). And they [the cold-blooded church under the Old Covenant] succeeded in their dastardly plan by conspiring with the Roman government to crucify Him. He was *"despised and rejected,"* *"a man of sorrows and acquainted with grief . . . wounded, afflicted, stricken and smitten of God."* Yet He was faithful to fulfill the great task assigned to Him by His Father: He *"bore our griefs and carried our sorrows . . . was wounded for our transgressions . . . bruised for our iniquities . . . [beaten and bruised] for our healing"* (Is. 53.1-12).

Even in His darkest hour in Gethsemane, His disciples chose rather to sleep than to tarry one hour with Him during His great agony of soul. He said to them, *"What, could ye not watch with Me one hour?"* (Mt. 26.40). His heart was broken by the rejection and callousness of His kinsmen after the flesh; He was *"contradicted of sinners,"* that is, by the whole human race; yet He graciously endured it! While on the Mount of Olives overlooking Jerusalem, He reflected, saying,

"O Jerusalem, Jerusalem, thou that killest the prophets, and stonest them which art sent unto thee, how often would I have gathered thy children together, even as a hen gathereth her chickens under her wings, and ye would not" (Mt. 23.37; Lk. 13.34).

Finally, He was even forsaken by His Father for a *"small moment."* He suffered and endured the Cross alone: crying out from the depths of His loneliness and passion, Eli, Eli, lama sabachthani *["My God, My God, why hast forsaken Me?]"* (Ps. 22.1; Mt. 27.46). And during this pitiful scene, we are told that *"it pleased the LORD to bruise him; He hath put Him to grief: when thou shalt make His soul and offering for sin . . ."* (Is. 53.10).

Now, observe; What is said here of Christ applies in some degree to all believers: and more especially to God's *"peculiar people"*—the church—the very *"Zion of the Holy One."* We must suffer, die, and be resurrected in Christ, both spiritually and physically (Rom. 6.1-6; Col. 3.1-3). Like Christ, we are perfected by the things we suffer. No cross, no crown! No pain, no gain! No suffering, no glory! Suffering is a mark of the true church! (1 Cor. 9.25; 2 Tim. 4.8; Jas. 1.12; 1 Pet. 5.4; Rev. 2.10). Hear the apostle, *"Yea, and all that will live godly in Christ Jesus shall suffer persecution"* (2 Tim. 3.12). Recall Jesus' words,

> *"And ye shall be hated of all men for My name's sake: but he that endureth to the end shall be saved . . . The disciple is not above his master . . . It is enough for the disciple that he be as his master, and the servant as his lord. If they have called the master of the house Beelzebub, how much more shall they call them of his household"* (Mt. 10.22-25).

Listen again to the apostle speaking to the church:

> *"Who now rejoice in my sufferings for you, and to fill up that which is behind of the afflictions of Christ in my flesh for His body's sake, which is the church"* (Col. 1.24; see also Phil. 1.29; 3.10-11).

We suffer in many ways, all of which works toward our perfection: through trials and persecutions, through afflictions and pains, through hardships and disappointments, through sicknesses, through backstabbing by pretentious friends and false accusers; in privations, in sore straits, in calamities, in labors, sleepless nights [watchings], in hunger [forced fastings]; and in necessities: even at times for want of food and sleep! (2 Cor. 6.4-10). Yet in all these things Paul was rather elevated than deflated! He was caught up into paradise, heavenly places in Christ Jesus, and heard things not lawful for a man to utter (12.1-10).

We are admonished therefore to equip ourselves with the mind of Christ (Phil. 2.5), namely, to humble ourselves under persecution and suffering to be exalted and to magnify the Lord. We should expect, therefore, to be abandoned, chastised, and afflicted, and to experience anguish and grief! When David said, *"Why art thou cast down, O my soul? Why are thou disquieted in me!"* (Ps. 42.5, 11), he was in *"the spirit of prophecy"* echoing down thru the corridors of time the groanings and passion of Christ. David's testimony was the testimony of Christ: for *"the testimony of Jesus is the spirit of prophecy"* (Rev. 19.11), that is, Christ was giving His own testimony through David.

And now He is giving His testimony through His church. We see, then, that if we desire to reign with Christ, we must also suffer with Him! (1 Tim. 2.12; 3. 10-12; 1 Pet. 4.1-2; Rev. 2.26-27). Like Jesus, we too must cry out to God in anguish of soul, in our suffering and affliction. God lets us sink deep into *"fiery trials"* and in our loneliness and separation from Him: so that we might more sincerely and deeply call upon Him for help and strength.

"Deep calleth unto deep!" It is *"our souls"* crying out to *"our God,"* and *"our God"* crying out to *"our souls!"* We see this in the lives of the prophets, like Job in his great anguish, and Jonah in the belly of the *"great fish."* Both men were purged and perfected through their suffering.

Now behold: the transcendent attributes of God are deep. He is everlasting, ever living, self-existent. He is omnipresent. His *"circumference is everywhere, His center nowhere." "[He sits upon] the circle of the earth"* (Is 40.22). His presence fills the cosmos, and

He exists beyond the created universe: for He spoke the universe into existence—*creatio ex nihilo* ("created out of nothing"). His intelligence and wisdom are infinite. God has never learned anything! Everything He knows now He has always known.

> *"Canst thou by searching find out God? Canst thou find out the Almighty unto perfection? It is high as heaven; what canst thou do? Deeper than hell; what canst thou know? The measure thereof is longer than the earth, and broader than the sea"* (Job 11.7-9).

His understanding and powers are infinite. He is limitless. Illimitable! Nothing is impossible to Him that is consistent with His nature and the laws He has established for the physical universe; which is to say, God cannot lie or steal or cheat; neither can He create dry water, or a square circle, or make a rock so great that He cannot move it (Gen. 1.1; 17.1; Is. 40.12-15; Jer. 32.17; Ezek. 10.5; Mt. 19.26; Rev. 15.3; 19.6; et al). But He can do anything consistent with His nature and reason.

Notwithstanding, the New Testament Scriptures speak more about the immanent attributes of God than the transcendent; especially those attributes that speak of the infinite depths of His person—of His heart and inner being, particularly in Christ who is the *"express image of His person"* and the embodiment of the whole Godhead (Col. 2.9; see also Jn. 14.6-10; Heb. 1.1-3; Rev. 1.8). Here is the mediating ministry of Christ, the Redeemer, opening the way [giving access] into the bottomless depths of the eternal Father (Jn. 10.30; 14.1-6; Rom. 11.33-36): the One who *"so loved the world that He sent His only begotten Son"* to save perishing humanity from eternal wrath (Jn. 3.16, 36; Eph. 2.3-7; Ps. 51.1-12).

God calls us from the depths of His heart! His work in salvation is deep! The Atonement is deep! The sacrifice of Christ is deep! Divine forgiveness is deep! His loving kindness is deep! His holiness and justice are deep. Just as we find it necessary so often to chastise our children, so God chastises His children. His love will not allow

Him to spare the rod of correction! He is not willing so easily to let us go astray. Accordingly, if we are without chastisement, we are not children of God. God chastises for our good (Heb. 12.10): for chastening purges and perfects us; it draws us closer and encourages intimacy with God, or rather it drives us to repent and seek forgiveness to be reconciled with God. The Cross provides the Way for reconciliation. Here is *"Deep [calling] unto deep!"*

We are driven by adversity to the foot of God's throne to inwardly reflect on our sins and/or our shortcomings. Repentance and reconciliation happen when the Deep meets the deep! When *"my soul"* and *"my God"* meet. Christ needed not to repent but was driven to His knees before His Father to get strength enough to endure the trials and afflictions that came against Him. He needed divine help to overcome the onslaught of demonic powers (Mt. 4.1-11; Lk. 11.18-22; Eph. 6.10-12).

"Who in the days of His flesh, when he offered up prayers and supplications with strong crying and tears unto Him that was able to save Him from death, and was heard in that He feared; Though He were a Son, yet learned He obedience by the things which He suffered; And being made perfect, He became the author of eternal salvation unto all them that obey Him" (Heb. 5.7-9).

Jesus needed supernatural strength to deal with His is infinite love for man anguish of soul—of separation and seemingly broken fellowship with God; of being diminished of God's presence and lacking intimacy with Him. Of being perceived as forsaken of God. That was more tormenting than physical pain. *"[tears were his meat day and night]." "My soul doth cry out!"* The feeling of being diserted and abandoned by His friends and especially by His heavenly Father drove Him to seek His face and plead for mercy. *"Deep calleth unto deep."* The depths of His soul calling for the depths of His Father to answer. So, the Lord calls from the depths of His being for all His children to be reconciled to Him. *"O Jerusalem, Jerusalem . . . how oft would I have gathered thy children together, even as a hen gathers her chickens under her wings, and ye would not!"*

At the same time, the Father and Son send the Holy Ghost to convict sinners of their iniquity and to reveal His love and mercy to them in forgiveness. They must be brought to the point of absolute dependence on God; to the understanding that there is no other name or power under heaven that can redeem and cleanse and restore a soul in the image of God. Through all the trials, temptations, chastisement, and anguish of soul, sometimes because of sin, sometimes because of weakness, true believers, like David, cry out for deliverance; in the deepest part of their soul, they believe the goodness and love of God will forgive and reconcile them deep within His bosom!

We cannot negotiate our own salvation; rather we repent and surrender to His pleadings with our souls. We court His favor. We meet God on His terms. For to have perfect peace, and feel the power of His justification, we must surrender all to His will. We must say, like Jesus when He was facing the cruel Cross on Golgotha, *"Nevertheless, not My will but Thine be done."* To be finally saved we must be willing to forsake all to follow Him, to die in Christ to live eternally (Mk. 8.34-38).

"I Surrender All"

Now observe: Christ gave up His heavenly status with God; left behind His cosmic glory to take on our humanity, with all its limitations and weaknesses. He *emptied Himself* [*"made Himself of no reputation"*] (Phil. 2.5-7); laid aside His divine prerogatives, became a man, a servant. As such, He took on sinful flesh, *"yet without sin"* (Rom. 8.3; Heb. 4.15), so that as man He could redeem men and reconcile us to God. He took on our poverty that we might partake of His glorious riches (2 Cor. 8.9; Jn. 17.20-23). In this sense, His greatest humiliation was not that He was crucified, but that He was born!

We learn humility from Jesus' example and the benefits of suffering from Him. Like Christ we are perfected through suffering. We are ordained to reach perfection, but we cannot get there except through suffering. Suffering is the vehicle that carries us to our perfection. When we perfectly consecrate ourselves to the Lord, our soul is taken by the Holy Ghost into the very depths of God, and at the same instance, into *"heavenly places in Christ Jesus"* (Eph. 1.3, 20; 2.6; 3.10-12). This is what Jesus prayed for: perfect union with the Father and the restoration of heavenly glory (Jn. 17. 5-10, 20-26). His desire for us is to inherit through Christ that same glory! In Christ we are taken up into God, into His inner sanctum, the *"Holies of Holies"*— the very depths of the Godhead. There we are immersed into His holiness and glory (Rom. 6.1-6; 2 Cor. 3.17-18; Gal. 2.20; 5.24; and see Heb. 9.7-28; 10.19-22; Mk 8.34-38).

In our text passage, David typifies Christ in his want of a heavenly state with God. The fallen angels had left their first estate, for God had cast them down with Satan (Jude 6; 2 Pet. 2.4; Rev. 12.7-10); but here Christ left His first estate willingly—an eternal and infinite state in which even the angels admired and worshipped Him. He left His first estate not for selfish reasons but because He so loved His Father and His plan to save fallen humanity.

"God sent His only begotten Son": yes, but also, in an unspeakable mystery He entered with Him in His suffering and crucifixion. *"God was in Christ, reconciling the world unto Himself"* (2 Cor. 5.18-19).

We noticed above that we must suffer with Christ if we expect to share in His glory, and be willing to endure our cross to live and reign with Him (Mk. 8.34-38). David's sufferings in Ps. 42 were in many ways a prototype of Jesus' sufferings and His struggles so that He might embody fully the perfections of His Father. In this Jesus served as a pattern for His church and all saints: for now *"[the ministry and word of reconciliation]"* has been committed to His church (2 Cor. 5.18-20). We now *"pray in Christ's stead"* and are *"workers together with Him"* (5.20; 6.1). And, like Christ, we are *"made perfect through suffering"* (6.4-10; Rev. 2.26-28; 2 Tim. 2.12).

We are admonished therefore to follow Jesus' example of humility and suffering *". . . to follow in His steps . . ."* (1 Pet. 2.21). He learned obedience by the things He suffered! (Heb. 5.8): and became a Son through His obedience and humiliation (1 Cor. 15.24-28; Phil. 2.3-11; Heb. 5.8). In turn, believers are called to follow and model Jesus' example. The LORD said, *"Do as I do!"* I have given you a divine pattern: *". . . an example, that ye should do as I have done unto you!"* (Jn. 13.15-17; see also Pet. 2.21).

Just as Jesus became the Anointed King of kings [by obedience and suffering], so we partake of the glory of His kingdom through obedience and suffering! (Acts 14.22; 2 Tim. 3.12). And just as God highly exalted Him by sharing His throne with Him (Phil. 2.9-10; 1 Cor. 15-24-28), so we also become kings and priests of God through obedience and suffering (1 Pet.2.9; Rev. 1.6; 5.10; 20.6), and will, accordingly, share with Him His throne in glory (Mt. 19.28; 1 Cor. 6.2; Rev. 2. 26-27; 3.21; 2 Tim. 2.11-12).

He became the Head of the church by obedience. We will become the bride of Christ through obedience. We are presently betrothed to Him, in the same way that Christ was something in-the-making; so are we. *"This day I have begotten you."* Jesus had been chastised and proven, so must we be chastised and proven (see Heb. 12.2-3)!

We must lose everything to gain heaven, even our very life! (Mk. 8.34-38; see also Gal. 2.20; 5.24; 6.14). We must be willing to be robbed of all but our God and our blamelessness (1 Cor. 1.8; Phil. 2.15; 1 Thess. 5.23; Titus 1.7). The Apostles' testimony must become our testimony, namely, *"Behold, we have left all to follow thee . . ."* (Mk. 10.28; see also Mt. 4.20, 22).

The Perfection of the Church

Psalm 42 is thus fulfilled first in David, a type of Christ; then in the incarnate Christ Himself during His life on earth. Then finally in God's church, the body of Christ, with all the saints. As such, we enter with Him into His whole experience as man. He was tempted and tried, mocked, humiliated, and forsaken. Yet all this worked for His perfection. He was purified like silver and gold in the fire (Mt. 20.20-23; Mk. 10.38-40, 45; Lk. 12.49-50). So must we also suffer to be purged and perfected! (Mal. 3.1-5; Mt. 3.10-12; Heb. 12.29; 1 Pet. 1.7; 4.12-19).

Again "life cannot be all sunshine!" Yes, we go *"from glory to glory"* but only *"through much tribulation"* (Acts 14.22; 2 Cor. 3.18; 2 Pet. 1.10-11). In between the precious moments of ecstatic joy, we must suffer and be afflicted, and necessarily so: for the glories become glorious only through times of darkness and trials and afflictions.

We experienced such a time in the late 1990s through April 2004, when the church was being purged and restored. We lost all to be faithful to the Lord and our God-given conscience: to regain what is most precious to us—fellowship with God in truth and holiness. We endured a *"great fight of afflictions"* to have perfect peace and joy and to be able again to rejoice in the prophetic vision of the church! Yes, much like David, we were deprived of our places of worship, exiled, marginalized, humiliated, scandalized, shunned, and scorned!

One of the often-used sayings of our former General Overseer, A. J. Tomlinson, when he was going through a stormy trial or affliction was, *"This is doing me good!"* This is how he saw his persecutions and suffering for the sake of the Gospel (Ps. 34.19; 132.1); he realized they all worked toward his perfection! It was so also with the apostle Paul. He saw his suffering as the way to obtain glory and eternal life:

"Most gladly therefore will I rather glory in my infirmities, that the power of Christ may rest upon me. Therefore, I take pleasure in infirmities, in reproaches, in necessities, in persecutions, in distresses for Christ's sake: for when I am weak then am I strong" (1 Cor. 12.9-10).

Accordingly, we *"count it all joy"* and patiently endure *"suffering affliction"* (Jas. 5.8-11): knowing that the end is the obtaining of His glorious kingdom! So, we sing, "Heaven will surely be worth it all!"

International Appointments
2021-2022

International Executive Council:

Wade H. Phillips, L.W. Carter, Scott E. Neill, Bruce Sullivan, Anton Burnette, Joseph A. Steele, Rick Ferrell [Council members were nominated by the Presiding Bishop and unanimously approved by the General Assembly.]

World Mission Director..Wade H. Phillips

Field Secretary..Ricky Graves

Mission Representatives..Jim Orange

Todd McDonald

Ambrosio "Roberto" Lopez

General Treasurer...America Wagner

Director of Education/School of Ministry Institute Director/Media Ministries Director..Anton Burnette

Shepherding Ministries Director.................................Wilma Carter

Assistant Publisher..Scott Neill

Fishers of Men Director...Bruce Sullivan

Ladies Ministries Director...Pamela Jones

Sunday School Director......................................Mandy Thompson

Sunday School Literature Editor..............................Bruce Sullivan

Children's Ministries Director....................................Kayla Graves

Executive Secretary/Receptionist.............................Wanda Busbee

Camping Coordinator/Youth Ministries Director.............Kim Erwin

Voice of Zion/SYNC Booster.......................................L.W. Carter

Senior Ambassador's Director..............................Donna Pounders

Tract Ministries Director...Glenda Major

Committees

Assembly Business Committee
Chairman: Zachary Snyder
Byron Harris, J.J. Davis, Tod Deakle,
David Gomba, Johanes Oboo

Doctrine Committee
Chairman: Bruce Sullivan
Trevor Graves, Joseph A. Steele, Tom Brown,
Yomi Adekunle, Allen Thompson

International Properties Committee
Chairman: Wade H. Phillips
L.W. Carter, Anton Burnette, Jim Orange,
Cecil Pounders, Glenda Major

General Trustees
Wade H. Phillips, Jim Orange, Anton Burnette,
Rick Ferrell, Alice Jones

Contact Information
International Executive Council

Burnette, Anton P.O. Box 2398, Cleveland, TN 37320; ph. 423-476-3337 or 423-716-5352; antonburnette@gmail.com

Carter, L.W. 60 Stayman Rd., Roanoke, VA 24019, ph. 540-597-8792; lwcarter43@hotmail.com

Ferrell, Rick, 105 Canterbury Dr., Crossville, TN 38558, ph. 615-670-1750; rsjsferrell@gmail.com

Neill, Scott E., 114 Ridge Rd., Greenville, SC 29607, ph. 864-420-4288; zascott@att.net

Phillips, Wade H. (Presiding Bishop), P.O. Box 2398, Cleveland, TN 37320; ph.423-476-3337 or 423-715-1091; presidingbishop@zionassemblychurchofgod.com

Steele, Joseph A., 1850 Strawhill Rd., Cleveland, TN 37323; ph. 828-226-8060; steeja@gmail.com

Sullivan, Bruce, 1141 Miller Rd., Greenville, SC 29607; ph. 864-419-2991; pastorbps@aol.com

International Staff

Burnette, Anton (Education Director, Media Ministries Director, School of Ministry Institute Director) P.O. Box 2398, Cleveland, TN 37320-2398 ph. 423-476-3337; antonburnette@gmail.com

Busbee, Wanda K. (Executive Secretary/ Office Assistant/*Voice of Zion* Layout & Design), P.O. Box 2398, Cleveland, TN 37320; ph. 423-476-3337; zionchurch11@bellsouth.net

Carter, L.W. (*Voice of Zion*/SYNC*)*, 60 Stayman Rd., Roanoke, VA 24019; ph. 540-597-8792; lwcarter43@hotmail.com

Carter, Wilma (Shepherding Ministries Director), 60 Stayman Rd., Roanoke, VA 24019; ph. 540-597-8792; lwcarter43@hotmail.com

Erwin, Kim (Youth Ministries Director and Camping Coordinator)
22 Hershel Davis Road, Drakesboro, KY 42337
270-977-6772; kimjerwin74@gmail.com

Graves, Kayla (Children's Ministries Director), 1140 Rogues Fork,
Bethpage, TN 37022; ph. 615-388-4643
childrensministries@zionassemblychurchofgod.com

Jones, Pamela (Ladies Ministries Director)
2850 Woodbury Loop, Morgantown, KY 42261;
ph.812-620-0052; pamjones938@gmail.com

Lopez, Ambrosio "Roberto" (Mission Representative)
13121 Chase Street, Arleta, CA 91331
951-999-2111; lopezrobert1969@gmail.com

McDonald, Todd (Mission Representative)
1010 Blythwood Drive, Piedmont, SC 29673
864.634.9315; tcmd@att.net

Major, Glenda (Tract Ministries Director), 118 Bullens, Ocoee
TN 37361; ph. 559-974-6574; GMAJORINC@AOL.COM

Neill, Scott E. (Assistant Publisher), 114 Ridge Rd., Greenville, SC
29607, ph. 864-420-4288; zascott@att.net

Phillips, Wade H. (Presiding Bishop, *Voice of Zion* Editor/ World
Mission Director), P.O. Box 2398, Cleveland, TN 37320;
ph. 423-476-3337; or 423-715-1091;
zionchurch11@bellsouth.net **or**
presidingbishop@zionassemblychurchofgod.com

Orange, Jim (Mission Representative)
443 Willow Creek Cove NE, Cleveland, TN 37323
615-477-2163; ojcorange@aol.com

Pounders, Donna (Senior Ambassador's Director)
1615 Dale Road, Caledonia, MS 39740
662-251-1270; pounderspainting.cj@gmail.com

Sullivan, Bruce (Fishers of Men Director/ Sunday School
Literature Editor), 1141 Miller Rd., Greenville, SC 29607
ph. 864-419-2991; pastorbps@aol.com
sseditor@zionassemblychurchofgod.com

Thompson, Amanda (Sunday School Director)
212 9th Ave. N., Amory, MS 38821; ph. 662-418-0809;
mandyt4@gmail.com

Wagner, America (General Treasurer)
226 McDonald School Road, McDonald, TN 37353
423-457-9504; americarosewagner@gmail.com

State Overseers
United States

North Carolina, South Carolina...................Scott E. Neill

West Virginia, Virginia
Pennsylvania, Maryland....................................J. J. Davis

Indiana, Kentucky, Illinois, Michigan.......................Ricky Graves

Tennessee, Georgia...Joseph A. Steele

Mississippi, Alabama, Louisiana...........................Zachary Snyder

Idaho, Wyoming...A.B. White

Kansas, Missouri, Colorado..................................Joseph A. Steele

Texas, Arizona, New Mexico..........................Samuel Hernandez

California, Nevada..Jose Manuel Lozano

Oregon, Washington............................Ambrosio "Roberto" Lopez

Contact Information
State Overseers

Davis, J.J. (**West Virginia / Virginia / Pennsylvania /Maryland**), 118 Bessie Ann Holl Rd., Farmington, WV 26571; ph. 304-365-0847; johnjdavis@gmail.com

Graves, Ricky (**Indiana / Kentucky / Illinois / Michigan**), 1995 Pleasant Grove Rd., Westmoreland, TN 37186; ph. 615-644-4127

Hernandez, Samuel (**Texas / Arizona / New Mexico**) 3733 Gannet Dr., Mesquite, TX 75181; ph. 214-4754285 hdzsamuel430@gmail.com

Lopez, Ambrosia "Roberto" (**Oregon / Washington**) 13121 Chase Street, Arleta, CA 91331; ph. 951-999-2111; lopezrobert1969@gmail.com

Lozano, Jose (**California / Nevada**) 15582 Lime St., Hesperia, CA 92345 ph. 310-365-5627; claudialozano89@gmail.com

Neill, Scott E. (**North Carolina / South Carolina**) 114 Ridge Rd., Greenville, SC 29607; ph. 864-424-4288; zascott@att.net

Snyder, Zachary A. (**Mississippi / Alabama / Louisiana**) 2357 Tahoe Drive, Mobile, AL 36695 ph. 574-8-49-6175; zs82@att.net;

Steele, Joseph A. (**Colorado / Kansas / Missouri**) 1850 Strawhill Rd., Cleveland, TN 37323; ph. 828-226-0227; steeja@gmail.com

Steele, Joseph A. (**Tennessee / Georgia**) 1850 Strawhill Rd., Cleveland, TN 37323 ph. 828-266-0227; steeja@gmail.com

White, A.B. (**Idaho / Wyoming**) 2801 Dove Ave., Apt.1228, Fairfield, CA 94533 ph. 707-980-0544; arlynnwhite@sbcglobal.com

United States
Churches/Missions/Pastors/Church Ministers

Amory, MS *(Church Minister)*......................Amanda Thompson
Anaheim, CA...Juan Avila
Arroyo Grande, CA..Moses Castillo
Bayou La Batre, AL...Tod Deakle
Beaver Dam, KY ....Todd Erwin
Bingamon, WV..Tom Brown
Browder, KY..Daren Childers
Caledonia, MS..Byron Harris
Coachella, CA..David Hernandez
Crossville, TN..Rick Ferrell
Cleveland, TN..Anton Burnette
Dallas, OR *(Mission)*...Kim Merrill
East Los Angeles, CA...Raul Carrasco Sr.
Fairfield, CA *(Mission)*..A.B. White
Flintville, TN *(Field work)*..................................Roger Barbour
Folsom, WV..Lee Brown
Fort Morgan, CO...Nazario Ornelas, Jr.
Fresno, CA *(Mission)*..Daniel Lucera
Goshen, IN..….........Charles Barker
Greenville, SC...Scott E. Neill
Hartsville, SC *(Mission)*....................................Jimmy Johnson
Hesperia, CA..Jose Lozano
Highgrove, CA..Pete Sarry
Idamay, WV..J.J. Davis
Jacksboro, TN...Ray Dickson
Karnes City, PA *(Church Minister)*.....................Brenda Reitler
Kingstree, SC *(Mission)*......................................Wayne Floyd
Lancaster, CA..Leyre Hernandez
Lompoc, CA *(Interim Minister)*.........................Priscilla Pompa
Lompoc, CA *(Prison Minister)*.............................Vicente Garcia
Madera, CA...Juan Lopez
Mesquite, TX...Samuel Hernandez

Oil City, PA *(Church Minister)*..................................Barbara Ion
Oxnard, CA.......................................Ambrosio "Roberto" Lopez
Pelzer, SC...Bruce Sullivan
Pulaski, TN...Joseph Steele
Rialto, CA...Fernando Fermin
Roanoke, VA...Dewey Gibson
Salisbury, MD..Joseph Quillen
Salton City, CA *(Field Work)*...............................David Hernandez
San Fernando, CA *(Mission)*............................Miguel Garcia, Jr.
San Jose, CA...Jorge Carrasco
Scottsville, KY..Trevor Graves
Sharon, WV *(Mission)*...Ron Massey
Taylors, SC *(Church Minister)*..........................Andrea Faye Davis
Visalia, CA *(Mission)*..Arthur Carillo
Ware Shoals, SC..Todd McDonald
West Mobile, AL..Zachary A. Snyder
Wilmington, NC..Robert Llaneza

Contact Information
United States Pastors

Avila, Juan (**Anaheim, CA**)
   9027 Stacie Lane, Anaheim, CA 92809;
   ph.714-313-4753; preacher4christ@gmail.com

Barbour, Roger (**Flintville, TN**/ *Field Work*)
   83 N. Vanntown School Rd., Flintville, TN 37335;
   ph. 931-993-0089; RDBarbour@yahoo.com

Barker, Charles (**Goshen, IN**)
   1306 E. 8th St., Mishawaka, IN 46544;
   ph. 574-361-5677; cdbarker58@comcast.net

Brown, Lee (**Folsom, WV**)
   2816 Mannington Rd., Smithfield, WV 26437;
   ph. 304-818-4642; leebrownlisa@gmail.com

Brown, Tom (**Bingamon, WV**)
   204 Buffalo Street, Mannington, WV 26582
   ph. 304-859-1055; bigamonchapel@gmail.com

Burnette, Anton (**Cleveland, TN**)
   P.O. Box 2398, Cleveland, TN 37320
   ph. 423-716-5352; antonburnette@gmail.com

Carrasco, Jorge (**San Jose, CA**)
   1901 O'Toole Way, San Jose, CA 95131
   ph. 408-605-2106; Bethinketh@gmail.com

Carrasco, Raul, Sr. (**South Central Los Angeles, CA**)
   9626 1/2 Kalmia Street, Los Angeles, CA 90002;
   ph. 323-477-6080; carrascocandy@yahoo.com

Carrillo, Arthur (**Visalia, CA** /*Mission*)
   3443 W. Sue Street, Visalia, CA 93277
   ph. 559-308-2871; zacog-centralcal@outlook.com

Castillo, Moses (**Arroyo Grande, CA**)
   905 N. East, Santa Maria, CA 93454
   ph. 805-314-5227; dodgers195981@gmail.com

Childers, Daren (**Browder, KY**)
   3559 Legacy Run, Owensboro, KY 42301
   ph. 270-903-9544; dardccool@live.com

Davis, John J. (**Idamay, WV**)
>118 Bessie Ann Hill Rd., Farmington, WV 26571
>ph. 304-365-0847; johnjdavis18@gmail.com

Davis, Andrea Faye (**Taylors, SC** *Church Minister*)
>61 Allen Rd., Travelers Rest, SC 29690
>ph. 864-979-2672; andreadavis0114@yahoo.com

Deakle, Tod (**Bayou La Batre, AL**)
>8365 Hemley St., Bayou La Batre, AL 36509
>ph. 251-327-7404; toddeakle@yahoo.com

Dickson, Ray (**Jacksboro, TN**)
>519 Mountain Rd., Clinton, TN 37716
>ph. 865-310-9181; ardickson12@yahoo.com

Gibson, Dewey (**Roanoke, VA**)
>5476 Catawba Valley Dr. Catawba, VA 24070
>ph. 540-598-9192; psgbeach74@gmail.com

Graves, Ricky (Interim) (**Beaver Dam**)
>1995 Pleasant Grove Road, Westmoreland, TN 37186
>ph. 615-670-4127; rgraves713@icloud.com

Fermin, Fernando (**Rialto CA**)
>353 South Riverside Ave., Rialto, CA 92376
>ph. 760-552-5381; fernandofermin4@gmail.com

Ferrell, Rick (**Crossville, TN**)
>105 Canterbury Dr., Crossville, TN, 38558
>ph. 615-388-8559; rsjsferrell@gmail.com

Floyd, Wayne (**Kingstree, SC**)
>24 Honey Path, Kingstree, SC 29556
>ph. 843-372-4336; jmfloyd40@hotmail.com

Garcia, Miguel, Jr. (**San Fernando Valley Mission**)
>8049 Bellaire Ave. N., Hollywood, CA 91605
>ph. 818-795-2443; zionofvalley.pastor@gmail.com

Garcia, Vincente (**Lompoc, CA - USP/FCI**)
>610 East Pine St. #68, Lompoc, CA 93436
>ph. 808-736-8553; alesiskorenko@yahoo.com

Graves, Trevor (**Scottsville, KY**)
>400 Parkway Dr., Scottsville, KY 42164;
>ph. 615-633-5347; trevorgravesmusic@yahoo.com

Harris, Byron **(Caledonia, MS)**
P.O. Box 284, Caledonia, MS 39740
ph.662-364-0136; parker3414@yahoo.com

Hernandez, David **(Coachella, CA)**
25273 Charity Court, Moreno Valley, CA 92553
ph. 909-452-0242; rh.davidhernandez1970@gmail.com

Hernandez, Leyre **(Lancaster, CA)**
43033 Carpenter Drive, Lancaster, CA 93535
ph. 661-916-6562; hernandezleyre@yahoo.com

Hernandez, Samuel **(Mesquite,TX)**
4612 Bonnywood Dr., Mesquite, TX 75150
ph. 214-475-4285; hdzsamuel430@gmail.com

Ion, Barbara **(Oil City, PA** *Church Minister*)
106 Ramer Dr. Apt. 105, Kittanning, PA 16201
ph. 724-525-9089

Johnson, Jimmy **(Hartsville, SC/*Mission*)**
1930 Long Branch Rd., Hartsville, SC 29550
ph. 843-861-4265; jimsfarm24@aol.com

Llaneza, Robert **(Wilmington, NC)**
5811 Fallen Tree Rd., Wilmington, NC 28405
ph. 910-632-4353; rllaneza@bellsouth.net

Lopez, Juan **(Madera, CA)**
921 Sonora St., Madera, CA 93638;
ph. 559-706-8617; juan10@yahoo.com

Lopez, Ambrosia "Roberto" **(Oxnard, CA)**
13121 Chase Street, Arleta, CA 91331
ph. 951-999-2111; lopezrobert1969@gmail.com

Lozano, Jose **(Hesperia, CA)**
15582 Lime St., Hesperia, CA 92345
ph. 310-365-5627; claudialozano89@gmail.com

Lucero, Daniel **(Fresno, CA)**
1544 E. Fedora Ave., Apt. 227, Fresno, CA
93704 ph. 559-837-7261; daniellucerozacog@gmail.com

Massey, Ronald **(Sharon WV*Mission*)**
P. O. Box 326, Dawes, WV 25054
ph.304-807-3101; rjmassey52@aol.com

McDonald, Todd (**Ware Shoals, SC**)
1010 Blythwood Dr., Piedmont, SC
29673; ph. 864-634-9315; tcmd@att.net

Merrill, Kim (**Dallas, OR/***Mission***)
818 Southeast Greenbriar Ave., Dallas, OR 97338
ph. 803-623-2915; rkmerrill@msn.com

Neill, Scott (**Greenville, SC**)
P.O. Box 16404, Greenville, SC 29607
ph. 864-420-4288; zascott@att.net

Ornelas, Nazario (**Fort Morgan, CO**)
629 Gayle St., Fort Morgan, CO 80701
ph. 970-217-0953; nornelas1953@gmail.com

Pompa, Priscilla (**Lompoc, CA** *Church Minister*)
935 Foxenwood, Orcutt, CA 93455
ph. 805-714-8028; prisnpompa@gmail.com

Quillen, Joseph (**Salisbury, MD**)
4901 Scotty Rd., Snow Hill, MD 21863
ph. 443-880-1659; jeanniequillen1660@gmail.com

Reitler, Brenda (**Karns City, PA** *Church Minister*)
324 Rose St., Mannington, WV 26582
ph. 330-283-0588; breitler53@hotmail.com

Sarry, Pete (**Highgrove, CA**)
12046 Preston St., Grand Terrace, CA 92313
ph. 951-237-2337; petes7573@yahoo.com

Snyder, Zachary A. (**Mobile, AL**)
2357 Tahoe Drive, Mobile, AL 36695
ph. 251-654-3201; zs82@att.net

Steele, Joseph (**Santa Barbara, CA** and **Missions**)
1850 Strawhill Rd., Cleveland, TN 37323
ph. 828-226-0227; jajrsteele@gmail.com

Sullivan, Bruce (**Pelzer, SC**)
1141 Miller Rd, Greenville, SC 29607
ph. 864-419-2991; pastorbps@aol.com

Thompson, Amanda (**Amory, MS** *Church Minister*)
1207 Concord, Amory, MS 38821
ph. 662-418-0809; mandyt4@gmail.com

National Overseers

Africa Central (*Mission Rep*)..................David Gomba
Africa West (*Mission Rep*)..................Yomi Adekunle
Argentina..................Jorge Estroz
Bangladesh..................Skuku Ranjon Sikder
Benin..................Saturnin Brice
Bolivia..................Yum V. Munoz Quispe
Burundi..................David Gomba
Cambodia..................Sam Bureenok
Cameroon..................Eyong Eric Eyong
Canada..................L.W. Carter
Chile..................Luis Alberto Martinez
Costa Rica..................Eugenio Cespedes
Democratic Republic of Congo..................Unduelo Byamungu Odo
Dominican Republic..................Saintaniel Hostelus
England (*Mission Rep*)..................Yomi Adekunle
Ghana..................David Dordah
Guatemala..................Ricardo Valenzuela Chavez
Guinea..................Philippe Seraphin Gomez
Haiti..................Saintaniel Hostelus
Honduras..................Nolvin Hernandez
India (South)..................V. Joseph Binoy
India (Mid-East)..................Talari Rao Padma
Kenya (North)..................Elijah Wafula
Kenya (South)..................Joanes Oboo
Malawi..................Maliele Dzuwa
Mexico (North)..................Danny Ramirez
Mexico (South)..................Ricardo Valenzua Chavez
Mozambique..................Maliele Dzuwa
Myanmar (Burma)..................Sam Bureenok
Nepal..................Raju Pariyar
Nicaragua..................Freddy Garcia
Nigeria..................Yomi Adekunle
Pakistan..................James C. Orange
Paraguay..................Jorge Estroz

Peru...Yum V Munoz Quispe
Philippines...............................Domingo Resurreccion
Rwanda (*Mission Rep*)...............................David Gomba
Sierra Leone...Joseph Alabi
South Sudan...…Elijah Wafula
Tanzania...David Gomba
Thailand..Sam Bureenok
Togo..Yomi Adekunle
Uganda......................................Maurice Ogada Odede
United States...Wade H. Phillips
Uruguay...Jorge Estroz
Venezuela...................................Bani Rangel Jimenez
Zambia (*Mission Rep*)...............................David Gomba
Zimbabwe (*Mission Rep*).........................David Gomba

Contact Information
National Overseers

Adekunle, Yomi: **Africa, West (*Mission Rep.*) / England (*Mission Rep*) /Nigeria / Togo**
P.O. Box 30769 Secretariat to state,
Ibadan to state Ibadan, Oyo 234, Nigeria; 2347033672742;
yomiadekunle2008@yahoo.com

Alabi, Joseph: **Sierra Leone**
ganiyi1977@yahoo.com

Binoy, V. Joseph: **India-South**
ZACOG in India, Valumannil Thombikandam P.O,
Ranni Makkapuzha Dist., Pathanamthitta, Kerala, 689676 India;
919544516258; zacogindia@yahoo.com

Brice, Gahou Saturnin: **Benin**
gahoubrice@gmail.com

Bureenok, Surisak: **Cambodia / Myanmar / Thailand**
145 MOO 10 BanTanod, Nakhonratchasima 30000 Thailand;
ph: 66-898445120; surisak_b@hotmail.com

Carter, L.W.: **Canada**
60 Stayman Road, Roanoke, VA 24019
ph. 540-597-8792; lwcarter43@gmail.com

Cespedes, Eugenio: **Costa Rica**
Oficina de Correos, Ciudad Colón, Mora, San José,
Costa Rica 10701, Costa Rica America Central;
ph: 50672836352; laverdadescritural@gmail.com

Chavez, Ricardo Valenzuela: **Guatemala / South Mexico**
Colonia La Repegua, Santo Tomas de Castilla, Puetro Barrios
Izabel, Guatemala 50245388494; ricardovchavez@hotmail.com

Dordah, David: **Ghana**
P.O.Box 643 WA, PLT 51 BLK "B",
Dobile-WA, Upper West Region Ghana +23321
ph: +233244840511; pastordordah@yahoo.com

Dzuwa, Maliele: **Malawi / Mozambique**
Area 36, P.O. Box 20151 Kawale Lilongwe, Malawi;
265999145597; dzuwamaliele@yahoo.com

Estroz, Jorge: **Argentina / Paraguay / Uruguay**
Juan D. Perón 148 Barrio Vista Hermosa, Centenario, Cp. 8309,
Neuquén Argentina; ph./Wassap: +54-299-5161022;
Fijo: +54-299-4896251; asambleadesionuruguay@hotmail.com

Eyong, Eric Eyong: **Cameroon**
P.O. Box 471, Fingo, Paradise Street, Kumba, South West Region, Cameroon; ph: +237-675936447; pastoreyong@yahoo.co.uk

Garcia, Freddy: **Nicaragua**
Managua Nicaragua Muncipil City; Sandino Bello Amaneer Zona 9; Quinte Calle Casa Q 469 Nicaragua 50586002898; 50586002898; freddygarcia@gmail.com

Gomba, David: **Africa, Central (*Mission Rep.*) / Burundi / Rwanda (*Mission Rep.*) / Tanzania / Zambia (*Mission Rep.*) / Zimbabwe (*Mission Rep.*) /**
P.O. Box 23, Shirati-Rorya, Mara, Tanzania East Africa; ph. 011255784599066; rucode_macademi2004@yahoo.com

Gomez, Philippe Seraphin: **Guinea**
Zion Assembly Church of God; BP: 121 N'zerekore, Conakry, Republic of Guinea; West Africa; ph.224628385727; wfjedu13@gmail.com

Hernandez. Nolvin Adolfo: **Honduras**
Colonialas Las Torres, Bloque 6 Casa 13, Choloma, Cortes, 21112, Honduras Central America; ph. 50495738697; nolvinhp@yahoo.com

Hostelus, Saintaniel: **Dominican Republic / Haiti**
Rue/Alexandre Petion, Bas-Aviation, Cap-Haitien Haiti; +50947787654; saintanielhostelus@gmail.com

Jimenez, Bani Rangel: **Venezuela**
Barrio Belle Monte, Casa 38A-585 Calle 128, Maracaibo Estado Zulia 4001, Venezuela; ph: 00584246725381; banirangel@gmail.com

Martinez, Luis Alberto: **Chile**
Esmeralda #60, Cobrico, Chile; ph. 952355637; luismartinez.1965@hotmail.com

Oboo, Joanes: **Kenya-South**
Box 18 Muhuru Bay, Kenya 40409; 254710560501; joanes.okal@yahoo.com

Odo, Unduelo Byamungo: **Democratic Republic of Congo**
Tel: +243 810855652; zionchurchdrc@yahoo.com

Ogada, Maurice Odede: **Uganda**
P.O. Box 29707; Kampala Uganda; 256785904643; mauriceogada2013@gmail.com

Orange, James C: **Pakistan**
443 Willow Creek Cove, NE, Cleveland, TN 37323;
615-477-2163; ojcorange@aol.com
Pariyar, Raju: **Nepal**
P.O. Box 86, District Post Office, Naurange, Bharatpur II,
Chitwan, Nepal; ph. 9779855052027; rajukhati@hotmail.com
Phillips, Wade H: **USA**
P.O. Box 2398, Cleveland, TN 37320, ph. 423-476-3337
zionchurch11@bellsouth.net
Quispe, Yum V. Munoz: **Bolivia / Peru**
Asosacion War Accopampa, WARI ACCOPAMPA, Mz. N.
Lt. 10-2, Ayacucho, Perú; ph. 966807780;
ymq_777@hotmail.com
Ramirez, Danny: **Mexico-North**
661 South Magnolia Ave., Rialto, CA 92376; 9095181271;
ramirez3134@sbcglobal.net
Resurreccion, Domingo: **Philippines**
64 Kamuning St. Amporo Subd., Calooca City 1400 Philippines;
ph: 09493421566; domres2004@yahoo.com
Sikder, Skuku Ranjon: **Bangladesh**
Village: Kaligram. P. O. Jalirpar District, Gopalgonj,
Bangladesh; ph. 880-01916036712; suku_clb@yahoo.com
Talari, Padma Rao: **India-Mid-East**
Rock Church Naidu Street, Bapunagar Rd., Nuzvid, Krishna
District, Andhra Pradesh, 521201, South India;
ph. 91-8008373847; 91-8656 796888;
bathanychurch@yahoo.com, rockchurch3@yahoo.co.in
Wafula, Elijah: **Kenya-North / South Sudan**
P.O. Box 3978 NCPB-Charenganni, Rift Valley Kitale, Kenya,
ph. 254722672323; welijah2000@yahoo.com

International Churches/Missions

Nation/Provinces	Churches	Missions
Argentina	7	1
Bangladesh	6	5
Benin	2	1
Bolivia	1	0
Burundi	2	1
Cambodia	1	0
Cameroon	5	3
Canada	2	0
Chile	7	2
Costa Rica	7	5
Dominican Republic	21	0
Democratic Republic of Congo	31	6
England	1	1
Ghana	1	1
Guatemala	21	10
Guinea	2	1
Haiti	234	0
Honduras	7	15
India Mid-East	17	16
India South	29	5
Ivory Coast	1	1
Kenya (North)	40	16
Kenya (South)	13	2
Liberia	1	1
Malawi	112	7
Mexico (North)	2	3
Mexico (South)	4	2
Mozambique	38	1
Myanmar	2	4

Nepal	26	1
Nicaragua	8	2
Nigeria	56	8
Pakistan	(contacts)	
Paraguay	1	0
Peru	1	1
Philippines	8	8
Rwanda	0	1
Sierre Leone	1	0
South Africa	(contacts)	
South Sudan	5	1
Tanzania	74	3
Thailand	4	12
Togo	1	1
Uganda	2	2
United States	40	8
Uruguay	1	0
Venezuela	12	1
Zimbabwe	3	1
Zambia	(contacts)	
	860	**160**

In addition to the above statistics, the church has 1,114 ministers and 76,119 members in 48 nations and provinces. Some members exist in nations where no church has yet been established. The church is also supporting 468 orphans in 5 orphanages in four countries (India, Kenya, Thailand, and Nigeria).

Licensed Ministers

Bishops

Adekunle, Yomi
Adelere, Adediran Solomon
Avila, Juan
Burnette, Anton
Carter, Lanny Woodrow
Chavez, Ricardo Valenzuela
Clement, Erasto
Davis, John Joseph
Dzuwa, Maliele Benesi
Espinoza, Ernesto
Fermin, Fernando
Ferrell, Rick
Ganda, Kenneth
Garcia, Miguel, Jr.
Gomba, David
Graves, Ricky
Harris, Byron
Hernandez, Nolvin Adolfo
Hostelus, Saintaniel
Jones, William
Kelton, Clifford
Lozano, Jose Manuel
Massey, Ron
McDonald, E.A.
McDonald, Todd
Misago, John Karegea
Neill, Scott E.
Oboo, Joanes Okal
Perez, Javier Patricio Diaz
Phillips, Wade H.
Quillen, Joseph D.
Ramirez, Daniel
Resurreccion, Domingo
Sarry, Pete
Sebukoto, Audax Petro
Snyder, Zachary A.

Steele, Joseph A.
Sullivan, Bruce
Wafula, Elijah
Webster, Davis
White, A.B.

Deacons

Akara, Vincent O.
Ashley, Dave
Carassco, Sam
Castro, Jace Amilcer Barnica
Clary, Kevin
Creary, Nevil Sena
Davis, Clyde (Eddie)
Davis, Jimmy
Dickson, Ray
Everett, Patrick Meredith
Ezakiel, Paulo
Gibson, Dewey Allen
Green, Joseph Leamon (J.L.)
Jaramillo, Robert
Jua'rez, Quilmer Javier
Llaneza, Robert
Martinez, Luis Acberto
Marwa, James
Mapambano, Stivin
Mlengera, Meshak
Monday, Sam
Moore, Larry Wayne
Murillo, Santos Fermin
Nyambaso, Kisyeri
Odoyo, Alfanyo
Okoth, Elisha
Okongo, Elphace
Omity, Makori
Omwando, Peterson O.
Onwaga, Joash Odongo

Oombo, James Opany
Orange, James C.
Reid, William
Rodriguez, Reny Naun
Spicer, Chad

Male Evangelists

Abeka, Daniel
Abura, Lazaro Orango
Achacha, Julias
Adebayo, Según
Adegboyega, Idowu Israel
Adebowale, Elijah Idili
Adera, John Odhiambo
Aderemi, Aderoju Timothy
Agbe, Nyakou
Agullana, Arnel Ganno
Agwanda, Joash
Akali, Ezakia
Akilolu, Taiwo Francis
Akuom, Sulman O.
Akwanya, Gerald
Alanya, Michael
Alfredo, Robert B.
Aluodo, Richard
Amando, Julio
Amos, Adetokun
Armand, Behanzin A.
Aremu, Abraham
Auyo, Juliias Myereere
Ayobami, Sanni Olusegun
Awiti, Daniel Oshiambo
Bagonle, Adebowak Elijah
Ballios, Jorge Antonio
Bamidele, Ademibawa Moall
Banvelos, Ambrosio "Roberto" Lopez
Barbour, Roger
Barker, Charles D.
Benjamin, Ammana. China

Betin, Akpatcho
Bienvenu, Oueni
Brown, Tom
Brown, Brooks Lee
Bundgere, Daniel Eliaz
Bureenok, Surisak
Brunet, Ricky Paul
Carrasco, Sr., Raul
Carrasco, Jorge
Carillo, Raul Arthur
Castillo, Moses Tarin
Castro, Esmerin Francisco Moncada
Catig, Teofilo
Corrales, Eugenio Cespedes
Chamorro, Vidal Morinigo
Chandra, Murala Surya
Childers, Daren
Christophe, Essee
Coello, Jose elis Orlando
Cook, Joseph Norris
Cespedes, Eugenio
Cortez, Carlos Jesus
Cortez, Luis Orlando
David, Oyadokun Olatundo
David, Samuel C.
Deakle, Tod
Diram, Joseph Oje
Dogbeda, Nouwe Kami
Dominguez, Gregorio
Duba, Ratna Babu
Ebenezer, Adebiyi Oluseye
Edward, Orobosa Kelly
Elisha, Chokka
Emanuel, Abioye Aladimeji
Espinoza, Carlos Adan Garcia
Esse, Chritop
Estacio, Mario
Etta, Silas
Everett, Patrick Meredith
Eyong, Eric Eyong
Felix, Kentangie John

148

Fermin, Fernando
Fikiri, Daniel
Floyd, Allen Wayne
Fredic, Duniani Asukulu
Gaba, Elias
Galvan, Nestor
Garcia, Alejandro
Garcia, Ivan Freddy
Garcia, Vincente
Garcia, Vitalino Martinez
Geda, Janes A.
Gomez, Luis Orlando
Gomez, Philippe Seraphin
Gonzales, Arthur
Gonzalez, Ruben Dario Fleitas
Granados, Marcos Caralino Galvez
Graves, Trevor
Graves, Travis
Green, Daniel Ray
Gregory, Daniel
Gregory, Jonathan
Gwara, Tom
Haleluya, Martin
Harvey, Tommy John Jr.
Hernandez, Leyre Josue
Hernandez, Nolvin
Herndanez, Samuel
Heunul, Juan Sergio (Paillaleo)
Ignacio, G. Benjamin
Ignacio, Ernesto
Ignacio, Melchor Gundran
Israel, Adebaye Oluwasagun
Israel, Koumako
Jaramillo, Alex Raymond
Jaramillo, Robert
Jandura, Godwin
Jaoka, Juma
Johnson, James, Jr
John, Felix Kentangie
Joseph, Okello Nabii
Juma, Eluis

Kagose, Peterlis
Kanydere, Simion William
Kayode, Oluwadepo Isaiah
Kelly, Greg
Kumar, Boddu Arunodaya
Lacorte, Jerry Seneres
Lagos, Mario
Lwe'ya, Yakobo Etumbedcho
Llobrera, Alejandro G.
Llobrera, Alvin
Lopez, Aminabel
Lopez, Juan
Lopez, Virgilio Amador
Lopez, Francisco
Lopez, Nicolas Daiz
Lourdes, La Cruz Martinez
  Sandra
Lucero, Daniel Ray
Lumbly, Samuel G.
Lwamba, Justin
Mabombe, Daudi
Mabula, Paulo
Mafuru, Alex
Magare, Ondigo
Maliyamungu, Michael Barnaba
Maliyamungu, Paskal
Moncada, Blas Efrain
Mang'ira, Antinius
Mansilla, Leonardo Simon
Martinez, Luis Alberto
Masese, Antonius Minira
Matabaro, Sylvester Fansisco
Mathayo, Allex
Mchura, Joseph
Mellado, Luis Alberto Martinez
Mendes, Feri Joel Martin
Miduda, Vitalis
Miruka, Amos Otieno
Mlengera, Meshak
Mnyangala, Michael Barnaba
Montecinos, Carlos Amador

Morgan, Nigel
Morakinyo, Ariwajoye Thomas
Morinigo, Maria Sirila Acosta de
Moses, Adebayo Kayode
Muga, William
Myodonga, Frederick Ochali
Ndosh, Daudi
Nkhwangwa, Agnostino Andre
Nunez, Carlos Agusto
Nyanjerechi, Jeremia
Nyodongo, Frederick
Oberio, George Otineno
Obiero, Mourice
Obuntmehin, Nathaniel
Ocando, Carlos Javier Govea
Ochanda, John
Ochola, Patrick
Ochola, Simon
Odede, Maurice Ogada
Odhiambo, Tom
Odo, Unduelo Byamungu
Odongo, Michael
Odongo, Moses Okoko
Ogbebo, Franklin Emokpea
Ogira, Ezra Ochola
Ogla, Bernard Otieno
Ogola, Lawrence, Oluoch
Oguntore, Samuel Bamikohh
Ogunleye, Peter Fowrunso
Ojetunde, John Owseye
Ojwang, Peter Otieng
Oketch, John Okoth
Oketch, Joseph Ombajo
Okeyo, Steve O.
Okimyi, Kigina Daniel
Okinyi, Florence Aoko
Okode. Jane Akinyi
Okong'o, Samwel O.
Okong'o Silas
Okoth, Simon
Okumu, Joshua

Olaide, Adebayo Kehinde
Oldyede, Aderibgbe Babatumde
Olal, Moris Anyanga
Olal, Michae Ngome
Olawuyi, Adekunle
Oloo, Almas Olouoch
Olubenga, Oyeyemi Gabriel
Oludare, Ayeni Moses
Olufemi, Olagunju Issac
Olusola, Adeleye Jonathan
Ombalo, Michael
Ombeta, Paul Odonyo
Omity, Makori
Omondi, Fred
Onesi, Matthew Bayode
Onyango, Joshia
Onyango, Philip Tel
Ooko, Agnes
Opiyo, Lukas
Ornelas, Jr, Nazario
Origi, John
Orwa, George Ohola
Osewe, Bernard
Osobu, Dotun
Otieno, Boaz
Otieno, Francis
Otieno, Okello
Otumba, Julias A.
Ouma, James Ng'anda
Ouyo, Julias Myerere
Oweri, Julias
Owiti, Syprose
Oyando, Eucabet
Oyediran, Timothy T.
Owewale, Asifat
Oyonge, James M.
Ozuda, Isaiah Omonid
Pailahueque, Jorge Enrique
Pariyar, Raju
Parker, James
Pastran, Manuel Antonio

Paulasa, Jorge Mario
Perez, Gladys
Perez, Leonardo Mendez
Pounders, Bobby
Powell II, Ryan Keith
Prakash, Yannabathula
Punda, Mika O.
Quezada, Sofanor
Quillen, Joseph
Quiroz, Mario Antonio Acevedo
Quispe, Yum Munoz
Rajoro, Peter
Ramirez, Hernandez Jonathan
Rangel, Ezequiel del Carme
Rao, Nimmala Sanjeeva
Rao, Talari Padma
Rao, Yadia Mohan
Ratnam, Sirra Mani
Reel, Jerry
Rodriguez, Carlos Rafael
Ruben, Perez Dario
Ruiz, Jose Dionicio
Saez, Mario Alfonzo Flores
Saka, John Onyango
Sakwa, Dan Ouma
Sakwa, Jack Obimbo
Sakwa, Jacob Obimbo
Samson, Akinlolu
Samson, Akinola Akinlolu
Sanchez, Antiono
Sanchez, Carlos Lopez
Sanchez, Pedro Danilo
Schroader, Jr., Daniel
Senapati, Gabriyel
Servellón, Manuel Francisco Sosa
Sikder, Skuku Fanjon
Solom, Pstyomi Adekunle
Solomon, George W.
Stephen, Ayoola Oloinka
Stonell, Raymond
Tabares, Werner

Taulinus, Fidel
Thompson, Allen
Tingler, Jerry
Tolentino, Jr, Federico D.
Torres, Cesar Augusto P.
Urcadiz, Daniel C.
Valdez, Wilmer Santos
Viswanatham, Biddika
Vicxeau, Jean
Wagner, Ricardo Astorga
Wale, Adeyemo Femi
Walowa, Joshua O.
Wambogo, Janes Mbaga
Wasse, Teketel Zewde
Wesley, Janga John
Wilcox, Bruce
Zuilenam, Guillermo Lienlaf

Female Evangelists

Adekumle, Yomi Olajumoke
Alabi, Opeyemi Elizabeth
Alfredi, Maria
Antango, Jane
Atieno, Monica
Badmus, Esther Olufunmilayo
Bolanio, Adejane J.
Cardenas, Blanca Esperanza
Chicag, Ana Gladys Martinez
Clardy, Dorothy
Daudi, Lensa
Davis, Andrea Faye
Dominguez, Dina Darleny Rodriquez
Dorcus, Oyediran Tunrayo
Daudi, Lensa
Duniani, Jeanne
Edward, Veline Nelson
Elizabeth, Ilesanmi Omodasola
Elizabeth, Alabi Opeyemi
Erasto, Rose, Atieno
Esther, Omotomilola Temitope
Erwin, Kimberly J.
Etando, Aziza
Faida, Rebecca
Fayoke, Asummo Omotola
Flores, Claudia Irene
Folasade, Ajayi Cecilia
Folasade, Osobu Paulina
Garcia, Irma Yolanda Martinez
Gonzales, Griselda Santigo
Grace, Sanni Iyabo
Gifford, Majorie
Ilesanmi, Mercy Olawunmi
Jandura, Memory D.
Jones, Pamela Lynn
Joseph, Dorkas
Joselyn, Treva
Kelton, Renetta Venise
Kimble, Shirley

Lopez, Dilcia Noris Villeda
Lwanba, Mwajuma
Maciel, Olga Beatrice
Matute, Gilma Leonor Dominguez
Michael, Issac
McKee, Ofelia
Morgan, Susan
Mojirayo, Taiwo Agnes
Motino, Santos Liliana
Obegoriola, Alarape
Obuyo, Damaris O.
Odhimago, Roseline Achiong
Ogonda, Joyce Adhiambo
Okumu, Elly
Olajumoko, Olaiya Olanike
Olu, Oladele Olukemi
Olufunke, Olujide Felicia
Olutunde, Adeyemi Joseph
Oluwa, Adebowale Janet
Omotunde, Durodola Adepeju
Ortiz, Celia Waldina Hernadez
Opakunle, Florence Tomi
Owira, Grace Auma
Perez, Gladys
Periera, Rebecca
Pinela, Margarita del Saez
Quillen, Jeannie
Quezada, Erica Pilar Pinto
Ramirez, Odalis Margoth
Reitler, Brenda
Rivera, Eva Yamileth Velasquez
Rivera, Yuliana Lizeth Velasquez
Romo, Reina
Sadler, Florence
Sanches, Marta Eloidina
Sandra, Lecruz Martinez
Sirrio, Janet
Snyder, Kari Elaine
Socia, Clarence
Stephenson, Tina

Suazo, Delmi Xiomara Matute
Suna, Susilia
Thompson, Amanda
Tomi, Opakunle Florence
Villafranca, Rosa Lidia Dominguez
Williams, Linda
Wilson, Nancy
Woldemichael, Eyerusalem W.

Exhorters

Burnette, Jonathan
Eldridge, Carl A.
Estrada, Cesar Augusto Estrada
Fields, Hayli
Floyd, Judi
Lupton, Kayla
Rodriguez, Henry
Wagner, Jacob

ABSTRACT OF FAITH

Note: The following has been accepted by the General Assembly in proper order, that is, by agreement in one accord.

Introduction

Zion Assembly is a Spirit-filled body of believers who have covenanted themselves together with God to accept and obey the teachings of Christ and His apostles (Ex. 19.3-6; Jn. 14.6, 8; Acts 2.42; Eph. 5.24-32). This commitment is firm, even in this present time of apostasy, when so many are *"falling away"* and *"[departing] from the faith"* (2 Thess. 2.1-12; 1 Tim. 4.1-3; 2 Pet. 2; 3.1-12; Jude 3-19).

The ministers and members of Zion Assembly have committed themselves to live and worship together in this *"most holy faith,"* to walk in truth, to *"endeavor to keep the unity of the Spirit in the bond of peace,"* and to cultivate among themselves the graces of love and holiness. They seek for the perfections of Christ in their fellowship, and by His grace and power to conform to the image of Jesus Christ so completely that when He appears they shall be like Him (Rom. 8.29; Col. 1.1-17; 1 Jn. 3.2).

Besides this internal disposition to cultivate mutual love and care within the household of God, the ministers and members have committed themselves to labor for the unity of all believers, until all *"see eye to eye," "speak the same thing," "walk by the same rule"* (Is. 52.8; 1 Cor. 1.10; Phil. 3.16). In this manner, they seek to carry forward the apostolic vision: *"Till we all come in the unity of the faith, and of the knowledge of the Son of God, unto a perfect man, unto the measure of the stature of the fullness of Christ"* (Eph. 4.13).

Zion Assembly has further obligated itself to publish and to proclaim the full Gospel into all the world in obedience to Christ's commission to the church (Mt. 28.19).

Church Membership

Membership in Zion Assembly is open to all believers whose testimony is evidenced by the fruit of the new birth, and who are willing to covenant themselves together with Christ and the church to walk in the light of the Gospel. Candidates become members by the following solemn obligation:

Will you sincerely promise in the presence of God and these witnesses, that you will accept this Bible as the Word of God, believe and practice its teachings rightly divided, with the New Testament as your rule of faith and practice, government and discipline, and agree to walk together as one body in the light of the Gospel to the best of your knowledge and ability?

In response to this covenant formula the candidate answers, "I will by the grace of God." The minister then lays hands on the new member and offers prayer for divine guidance and strength; the congregation follows with an affectionate welcome and extends the right hand of fellowship.

Prominent Teachings in the Scriptures

Note: *The following statements are not meant to form a creed, or to be thought of as an exhaustive statement of beliefs upon which the church is built. They are simply an abstract of some of the important and fundamental teachings and principles set forth in the Holy Scriptures, which form an essential part of the church's Rule of Faith.*

The Trinity—The Bible teaches that the one eternal God exists in three persons: namely, the Father, Son, and Holy Spirit. These Three have distinct identities, yet they form one undivided Godhead, subsisting in the same nature (Rom. 5.5; 15.16, 30; 2 Cor. 1.20; 5.19; Jn. 3.5; Eph. 2.18; Titus 3.5). The Father is God (Eph. 4.6), the Son is God (Jn. 1.1-3; 10.30; Heb. 1.8; Rev. 1.8), the Holy Spirit is God (Jn. 14.17; 16.13; Acts 5.3; 1 Cor. 2.10), yet there are not three Gods, but one God (Deut. 6.4). The three persons of the divine Trinity work together in perfect unity for the salvation of man (Jn. 3.5; 6.44; 14.6, 16-17; 2 Cor. 5.19).

Jesus Christ—Jesus Christ is the *"image of the invisible God"* (Col. 1.15), and God's *"only begotten Son"* (Jn. 3.16). Through Him,

God was manifest in the flesh, justified in the Spirit, seen of angels, preached unto the Gentiles, believed on in the world, received into glory, and now sits on the right hand of God to make intercession for us (Acts 7.55; 1 Tim. 3.16). Through Him alone men have access unto the heavenly Father. It is through His sacrificial and atoning death on the cross that we are saved. *"Neither is there salvation in any other: for there is none other name under heaven given among men, whereby we must be saved"* (Acts 4.12). He is the spotless *"Lamb of God, which taketh away the sin of the world"* (Jn. 1.29). He is also the head of the church and the savior of the body (Eph. 5.23).

Angels—The word angel means *"messenger."* Scripture teaches that angels are heavenly and supernatural beings, but also they are creatures (Col. 1.16; 1 Pet. 3.32). As such, they were created to worship God and do His bidding (Is. 6.3; Mt. 26.53; Heb. 1.6-7, 14; Rev. 4.8). Their nature is incorporeal; they are *"spirits"* (Heb. 1.14), created holy and with free will. As such, some fell from their *"estate"* (Jude 6). In regard to the time of their creation, we are not informed explicitly in Scripture, but a few passages indicate that they were created before man and were present when God created man (Gen. 3.1; Job 38.7). In their role as *"messengers,"* they have been commissioned by God to minister in the affairs of man (Heb. 1.13-14; Ps. 34.7). They exist in ordered ranks—*"principalities," "powers," "thrones," "dominions"* (Eph. 6.12; Col. 2.15), and also as "seraphim" and "cherubim." The distinctions between seraphim and cherubim are not made clear in Scripture (Gen. 3.24; Ezek. 10.1-3, 7-14; Is. 6.2, 6).

The "messenger ministry" of angels can be seen both in the Old and New Testaments (Judg. 6.11; 13.3; 1 Kgs. 19.5; Psalm 91.11; Lk. 1.11; Mt. 1.20; 4.11; 28.5). The Bible reveals that angels are great in number (Deut. 33.2; Dan. 7.10; Mt. 26.53; Lk. 2.13; Rev. 5.11) and have great power, intelligence, and supernatural ability to move with great speed. As such, man is said to have been *"made a little lower than the angels"* (Psalm 8.5). Notwithstanding, though angels are powerful, highly intelligent, and have great mobility, they are not all-powerful, all-knowing, nor omnipresent. (For example, they do not know when the Rapture will take place (Mt. 24.36).

As created beings, angels have a beginning, but they never die nor cease to exist (Lk. 20.36). Angels are not God or gods, and thus man is forbidden to worship them (Col. 2.18). In fact, the holy angels themselves [those who did not join in Satan's fall and rebellion] reject any attempt by man to worship them (Rev. 19.10; 22.28).

Angels cannot repent nor be redeemed from sin, and thus the fallen angels are doomed forever to damnation. Nor do angels act as Gospel evangelists in the work of salvation, this ministry being assigned to born-again believers and more especially to the church (Acts 10.3-6). Yet angels assist the church in its mission (Acts 10.3-7; 11.13-14; 8.26; 5.19-20; Heb. 1.14). Jesus informs us also that the holy angels rejoice at the redemption of sinners (Lk. 15.10).

Scripture teaches that one-third of the angels followed Satan in a great rebellion against God (Is. 14.12-15; Rev. 12.4, 7-9), and that they labor in this present age under Satan's rule to *"steal, and to kill, and to destroy"* (Jn. 10.10; Eph. 6.10-12). These fallen angels are referred to as *"evil spirits,"* *"unclean spirits,"* and *"demons,"* and thus Jesus spoke of *"the devil and his angels"* (Mt. 25.41; see also Rev. 12.7). They have been sentenced to a realm of darkness, and live with the dread of their final judgment in the Lake of Fire (Jude 6; Mt. 25.41; 8.29).

Unlike Adam and the human race, angels were not created as a race, and therefore when one-third of the angels fell under Satan's deception, all the angels did not fall with them. Each was created separately, and each fell by his free choice independently. Nor did Satan transmit his sin to the other angels; but rather deceived one-third of the angels into a rebellion against God; thus each angel sinned of his own volition. Further, unlike the human race, angels do not have sexual desires and do not procreate or reproduce (Mt. 22.30); neither were angels created, like man, male and female; and thus no angel in Holy Scripture is referred to as being female. It is important to understand also that Satan is not the God-ordained head of angels, but rather he assumed his position by deception and in rebellion against the will of God.

Finally, though men are clothed with heavenly bodies in glorification (1 Cor. 15.48-53) and in that glorious state share some angelic characteristics (Lk. 24.34-36), yet they do not become angels. The distinctions between men and angels will remain throughout eternity (Rev. 5.9-13).

The Bible—The Holy Scriptures, both Old and New Testaments, reveal God and His will for man. They are inspired, inerrant, infallible, and unchangeable (2 Tim. 3.14-16; 2 Pet. 1.16-21). The truths of the Scriptures are revealed by prophecy, type, precept, and example, illuminated through the power of the Holy Spirit. The teachings of the Bible, particularly in the light of the New Testament, are the church's final rule for faith, practice, government, and discipline (Acts 2.42; 2 Pet. 3.1-2). Walking in the light of God's Word is the guiding principle and commitment of Zion Assembly: *"Thy word is a lamp unto my feet, and a light unto my path"* (Psalm 119.105).

The Church is a visible body of believers formed and incorporated by covenant with God to keep His commandments (Ex. 19.5-8; 24.3-8; Ps. 119.57; Jn. 14.15; 17.6, 8, 14; 1 Pet. 2.9). It is theocratic in form and function, providing order and government through the Spirit and the Scriptures for God's people (Is. 2.2-4; 9.7; Mt. 18.15-20; 1 Cor. 12.28). The church is presently imperfect, spotted with backsliders and *"false brethren"* (1 Cor. 5.1-13; Gal. 2.4; Jude 4). It is thus distinguished from the kingdom of God, the latter being the spiritual realm of all born again believers (Jn. 3.3-8; Rom. 14.17; Col. 1.13). One is *"born"* into the kingdom; he/she is *"added to the church"* (Jn. 3.3-8; Acts 2.47). The church will succeed to proclaim the Gospel into all the world (Mt. 24.14; 28.18-20; Mk. 16.15-16); will be perfected *"with the washing of water by the word,"* and will be presented to Christ glorious in holiness (Eph. 5.26-27). The General Assembly is the highest tribunal of authority in the church for the interpretation of the Scriptures (Acts 15;1-16.4-5). The purpose of the General Assembly is to promote unity and fellowship among the saints, to search the Scriptures for additional light and understanding, and to resolve differences in interpretations which tend to be divisive among the ministers and churches. All matters of faith, government, and discipline are discussed before the entire body of the church assembled, and resolved in one accord with the manifest approval of the Spirit (vv. 12, 22, 28). This form and order is based on the precedent: *"For it seemed good to the Holy Ghost, and to us"* (Acts 15.28). All male members in good standing have an active voice in the Assembly. Women are a vital part of the church's life and ministry. In matters dealing with church authority, however, they voice their opinions through their husbands and/or church elders (1 Cor. 11.3, 7-9; 14.34-36; 1 Tim. 2.12; 3.1-17).

Man is unique in all of God's creation. Only he was created in God's image and likeness (Gen. 1.27; 5.2; Eccles. 7.29; 1 Cor. 11.7; Eph. 4.24), and therefore man has a unique relationship to God. His nature is composed of soul, spirit, and body (Job 32.8; Eccles. 12.7; Mt. 10.28; 1 Cor. 15.45; 1 Thess. 5.23; Heb. 4.12), though *"soul"* and *"spirit"* may be fully distinguishable only by the Spirit of God (Heb. 4.12 and compare Jn. 12.27 and 13.21). Of all the living things on earth, only man has God-consciousness and an immortal soul (Gen. 2.7; 1 Cor. 15.45). He thus has an everlasting destiny in heaven or hell, with eternal life or everlasting death and damnation (Rom. 6.23; Rev. 20.4-6; 21.7-8). He was created by divine decree in one day; he did not therefore evolve, nor does he exist by chance. Moreover, the uniqueness of man is seen in that he was given authority in earth over all living things including animal life (Gen. 1.26, 28). This uniqueness is partly why the Psalmist exults, *"I will praise thee; for I am fearfully and wonderfully made"* (Ps. 139.14), and why he asks, *"What is man, that thou art mindful of him?"* (8.3-4; Heb. 2.6).

Man was created *male* and *female* (Gen. 1.27; 2.18, 21-25) in order that the genders might come together under divine institution as husband and wife (Gen. 2.21-25; Mk. 10.6-9) to procreate the race of man—to *"be fruitful, and multiply"* (v. 28; 9.1)—and to provide comfort and companionship for one another (Prov. 18.22; Eccles. 9.9; Eph. 5.22-25, 28-31; 1 Pet. 3.7). This is the divine order for man, making *fornication* (pre-marital sex, homosexuality, incest, bestiality) and *adultery* (unfaithfulness in marriage, and divorce and remarriage while one's first companion is still living) vile corruptions of God's expressed will and design for man (Mal. 2.14-16; Mt. 5.28; Mk. 10.7-12; Lk. 16.18; Rom. 7.2-3; 1 Cor. 7.10-11, 39).

Included in man's God-consciousness is an innate sense of morality—of moral right and wrong—and a sense of accountability for his behavior (Acts 17.28-30; Rom. 1.19-20; Jn. 1.9). Moral responsibility and accountability are predicated on the nature of man's God-consciousness and free will, that is, his ability to choose and act in obedience or disobedience to God's revealed will (Josh. 24.15-25; 1 Kgs. 18.21; Ezek. 20.39; Lk. 13.35; Jn. 3.36; Rev. 22.17).

Man was created holy, in the moral image of God (Gen. 1.27; 31; 5.1-2), but his fall in Eden plunged him into sin and corruption. His fall was predicated on the fact that he has free will. Adam chose, under the influence of Satan's seductive power working through Eve,

159

to disobey God. Because man is a race, unlike the angels, sin was transmitted to all men through Adam's transgression (Gen. 3.6; Rom. 5.12; 1 Cor. 15.21). His redemption and reconciliation to God was made possible by the sacrifice of Christ (Rom. 5.15-19).

Christ is the second man Adam (1 Cor. 15.22, 45). He is therefore called the Son of Man as well as the Son of God (Mt. 12.8; 16.13; Lk. 1.35; Jn. 1.14; Col. 1.15, 19; Heb. 1.8; Rev. 1.8). In Him God and man exist in one person (Jn. 1.1-3, 14; Phil. 2.5-8). The first Adam failed and plunged man into sin; the second man Adam, Christ, lived triumphantly over sin (2 Cor. 5.21; Heb. 4.15), making it possible for us also to triumph over sin and be saved (Is. 53.4-9; 2 Cor. 2.14; 1 Pet. 2.21-24). He that believes and repents and is born again shall be saved (Jn. 3.3-8, 16; 10.28). Christ is the perfect man, and all men can be made perfect in and through Him, our redeemer and sanctifier (Heb. 2.11; 10.10, 14; 13.12).

Sin is a real and expressed evil. It originated in Satan in heaven (Is. 14.12-14; Jn. 8.42; 1 Jn. 3.8; Rev. 12.7-9), and in man in the Garden Eden when Adam rebelled and transgressed against God's explicit command and ate of the forbidden fruit (Gen. 3.6, 17). Sin is thus willful rebellion against the law of God (Ex. 35.19; Psalm 51.3; Heb. 4.7; 10.26; 13.18; 2 Pet. 3.5) It may be defined as *lawlessness* (Rom. 3.20; 4.15; 5.13; Gal. 3.19; 1 Tim. 1.9), *transgression* (Ps. 119.158; Eph. 2.1; 1 Jn. 3.4), *disobedience* (Rom. 8.7; Titus 1.16; 3.3; 1 Tim. 1.9; 1 Pet. 2.7-8), and *rebellion* (Psalm 78.8; Lam. 1.18; 3.14; Dan. 9.5). Sin exists also in unbelief (Jn. 3.18; Titus 1.15; 1 Jn. 2.22-24; Rev. 21.8).

Unlike the angels, mankind is a race; thus when the first man Adam sinned, sin was transmitted to all men through him (Rom. 5.12). All men are therefore born with the sin nature and therefore with the propensity to sin (Ps. 51.5; 58.3; Eph. 2.3; 1 Jn. 1.8). None are exempt, including Mary, the mother of Jesus. *"For all have sinned, and come short of the glory of God"* (Rom. 3.23).

Sin exists in two forms: **1)** in the very being of man, in his rebellious nature (Rom. 6.6; Eph. 2.3); **2)** in actual acts of transgression (Eph. 2.1; Col. 2.13). Sin is conceived in the heart and is expressed in thought (Gen. 6.5; Mt. 15.19), word (Mt. 5.22), and/or deed (Rom. 1.32).

Death and everlasting damnation is the penalty that God imposed upon mankind for sin (Rom. 6.23). The Good News is that the shedding of Jesus' blood, His death on the Cross, and His resurrection provided the remedy for sin (Rom. 5.15-19; Heb. 9.22). By grace, through faith in Christ, transgressions are forgiven and the *"old man,"* the sin nature, is crucified.

In justification, actual transgressions are pardoned and washed away (Rom. 3.28-30; 5.1; Eph. 2.5; 13-18); in sanctification, the very nature of sin rooted in man's heart is uprooted and removed (Rom. 6.6; Gal. 2.20; 5.24; 6.14; Col. 3.3-10). The sanctified believer is thus made free from sin (Jn. 8.36).

Works of the Flesh—The *"works of the flesh are manifest, which are these: adultery, fornication, uncleanness, lasciviousness, idolatry, witchcraft, hatred, variance, emulations, wrath, strife, seditions, heresies, envyings, murders, drunkenness, revellings, and such like"* (Gal. 5.19-21). The apostle Paul sets forth three general categories of carnality [*"works of the flesh"*]: **1)** sensual and sexual sins, which include adultery, fornication, immorality, impurity, unfaithfulness, and lewdness of all kinds, which may be committed before and/or during marriage; **2)** sins of spiritual deception and demonic seduction through false religion, which include idolatry, witchcraft, sorcery, divination, necromancy, magic, enchantments, palm readings, superstitious rituals of paganism, and new age teachings and practices; **3)** sins that stem from a malicious and spiteful spirit, which include hatred, enmities, wrath, strife, jealousy, uncontrolled anger, murders [actual or harbored in the heart], bitter disputes, dissensions, factions, heresies, seditions, envying, drunkenness, carousing, and ranting and rioting.

The list of the *"works of the flesh"* given by the apostle Paul in Gal. 5 is not a complete list of sins. There are many more subtle works of the flesh and of the spirit that are not so *"manifest"* or obvious, including greed, covetousness, stealing, extortion, gossip, slander, whisperings, and evil speaking. The apostle thus adds to his list of sins the words, *"and such like."* His point in bringing these sins to the attention of the church and identifying them in particular is to make us more conscious of the destructive nature of sin and to set forth God's remedy for sin in Christ. Deliverance from the powerful works of the flesh cannot be obtained through the law and practices of religion but only *"through sanctification of the Spirit"* and the Word of

God (Gal. 5.16-18, 24; 1 Thess. 5.23; 2 Thess. 2.13). The sanctifying power of Jesus' blood received by faith through the Holy Spirit is the remedy! The *"old man"* must be crucified in order for the believer to be made free from and victorious over sin (Jn. 8.36; Rom. 6.6; 8.1-6; Gal. 2.20; 5.24; 6.14; Eph. 4.22-24; Col. 2.11, 12). Further, the old man is kept crucified by our daily consecration and *"walk in the Spirit"* according to the Word of God (Gal. 5.16, 25; 2 Tim. 2.21-23).

Salvific Work of Grace

Conviction is a revelation to man by the Holy Ghost of the righteous judgment of God. Through conviction, unregenerated souls see themselves as sinners before God, experience guilt, and realize their separation from Him who is holy, just, and good (Is. 6.1; Jn. 6.44; Acts 2.37-38). True repentance can be made only through the work of the Spirit in conviction (Jn. 16.7-15; 1 Cor. 12.3; see also Jn. 8.32; 14.6).

Repentance is the act of confessing one's sins before God, being willing to forsake them and to turn to Christ with all of one's heart, mind, soul, and strength. True repentance can be made only in the spirit of *"godly sorrow"* (2 Cor. 7.9-10). Repentance is manifested by certain fruit *"meet for repentance"* (Mt. 3.8; Rom. 6.2). The act of repentance should be followed by water baptism [see page 19] (Mk. 1.4-5, 15; Lk. 13. 3; Acts 3.19; 5.30-31; 1 Jn. 1.9). Repentance is a prerequisite experience for justification.

Justification is the state of being void of offense toward God. It is made possible through the atoning blood of Jesus Christ. It is the act of God in forgiving the transgressions of a penitent sinner. Justification is the result of repentance and faith (Rom. 8.1-2; 3.23-26; 1 Jn. 1.7). The genuinely justified person has *"peace with God through our Lord Jesus Christ"* (Rom. 5.1-2). Justification signifies the pardon (forgiveness) aspect of the new birth.

Regeneration is the act of God in creating new life in the heart of the believer through the Holy Ghost. It is a definite and instantaneous experience. Man is dead in sins and trespasses through Adam and can be quickened or regenerated only through faith in Christ and His atoning sacrifice (Eph. 2.1, 4-5; Col. 2.13-14; Jn. 5.24). Regeneration is the same as the new birth. *"Born Again"* is another term for regeneration. The result of this experience is that the believer becomes a child of God. It is through this new birth that one becomes a part of the Kingdom of God. Jesus said: *"Ye must be born again"* (Jn. 3.3-8; 1 Pet. 1.23). The new birth is a prerequisite condition for the experience of sanctification.

Fruit of the Spirit is of divine origin. It is the very life of God poured into the heart of the regenerate believer. The fruit of the Spirit is love, joy, peace, longsuffering, gentleness, goodness, faith, meekness, temperance (Gal. 5.22-23). We are admonished in the Scripture to walk in the Spirit and not to fulfill the lust of the flesh (Gal. 5.16; Eph. 5.9; Phil. 1.11).

Divine Healing is provided for all in the atonement. Christ's atoning sacrifice on the cross provides healing for the whole man, including his body. Divine healing is effected by faith without the aid of medicine or surgical skills. In cases where one is healed through the assistance of physicians, medicine, herbs, etc., God is still to be praised: for it is God who heals in any case. *"Bless the Lord, O my soul, and forget not all his benefits: Who forgiveth all thine iniquities; who healeth all thy diseases"* (Psalm 103.2- 3; Is. 53.4-5; Mt. 8.17; 2 Pet. 2.24; Jas. 5.14-16).

Subsequent Grace

Sanctification is the second definite work of grace wrought in the regenerated heart by faith. In sanctification, the carnal nature is eradicated (*"the old man is crucified"*) so that the believer no longer has the inclination or propensity to sin; that is, in sanctification the desire to sin is removed (Heb. 10.10; 13.12-13; Rom. 6.1-6; 1 Thess. 4.3; 2 Thess. 2.13; 1 Pet. 1.2). Sanctification enables the believer to bring his/her body under subjection to Christ, and to live a life consistent with the spirit of holiness and in accordance with the Word of God. Sanctification is a prerequisite condition for the baptism with the Holy Ghost.

Holiness is the result of sanctification. It is a state of grace and purity in which perfect Christlikeness is desired and pursued (Mt. 5.48; 2 Cor. 7.2). God has called us unto holiness (Thess. 4.7). *"Be ye holy; for I am holy"* (1 Pet. 1.15-16). *"Follow peace with all men, and holiness, without which no man shall see the Lord"* (Heb. 12.14; see also Lk. 1.74-75; 2 Cor. 7.1; Titus 2.11-12; Eph. 1.4; 4.13, 24). Paul expressed his desire to *"present every man perfect in Christ Jesus"* (Col. 1.28). Christ is returning for a church that is glorious in holiness: *"without spot, or wrinkle, or any such thing"* (Eph. 5.27; see also Ps. 45.9-13).

Christian Perfection—The perfection of the believer is the call and aim of the Gospel (Mt. 5.48; Jn. 8.36; 2 Cor. 13.11; Col. 1.22; Heb. 6.1; Jas. 1.4; Jude 24). Redemption anticipates purification and perfection, and this state of grace is to be attained *"in this present world"* (Titus 2.11-14). Christ gave His life and shed His blood to make believers perfect in Him (Heb. 10.1, 14; 13.21), both individually and corporately in the body of Christ (Mt. 5.48; Jn. 17.20-23; 2 Cor. 13.9; Col. 1.28; Eph. 1.10; 2.14-22; 4.11-16; 5.27; Rev. 19.7-8). This glorious experience has therefore been called "Christian perfection," for it is attained in and through the grace of Christ by the Holy Spirit. The grace of perfection therefore glorifies God, not man.

Christian perfection is not the same as absolute perfection, for only God is absolutely perfect (Ex. 9.14; 1 Sam. 2.2; 1 Chron. 17.20; Job 11.7; Mk. 10.18). Thus Christian perfection is defined and explained in the Scriptures in ethical terms, rather than in legal terms; that is, Christian perfection is a state of grace attained through a perfect relationship with God. As such, it is rooted in and springs forth from *"perfect love"* (Mt. 5.44-48; 1 Cor. 13.1-13; 1 Jn. 2.5; 4.12, 17). Love is in fact the *"bond of perfectness"* (Col. 3.14). Christian perfection is therefore essentially grounded in love and wrought in the heart by the Holy Spirit (1 Chron. 28.9; 2 Chron. 15.17; 16.9; 19.9; Rom. 5.5; Heb. 10.22). Accordingly, a believer may err in mental judgments, be forgetful, be sick or afflicted physically, have moments of anguish and perplexity, etc., and yet not be charged with sin or willful rebellion and disobedience against God's will and law (Rom. 8.33; Eph. 4.26; Heb. 10.26). The human condition therefore does not necessarily militate against the saint's perfect relationship with God and with his fellow man.

There is, moreover, growth in sanctification and in perfection unto a more glorious state of perfection in Christ. Thus the saint is transformed ever more perfectly by the Spirit of God into the image of Christ *"from glory to glory"* (2 Cor. 3.18). Sanctified believers are admonished to continue to *"perfect holiness in the fear of God"* (2 Cor. 7.1). The Good News is *"we know that, when [Christ] shall appear, we shall be like him"* (1 Jn. 3.2; Eph. 5.27).

Perseverance reveals the grace imparted to a believer to live in obedience to the Gospel of Jesus Christ in spite of any opposition or hardship that may challenge his Christian faith (2 Tim. 2.3-4). Although the word *"perseverance"* is used only once in some translations of the Bible (for example, Eph. 6.18 in the King James Version) there are many other words that are closely related to it, such as *abide* (Jn. 15.4-5, 7-9), *endure* (Mt. 10.22), *continue* (Jn. 8.31-32), *steadfast* (Heb. 3.14, 1 Pet. 5.8-9, 2 Pet. 3.17), *patience* (Lk. 21.19), *overcome* (Rev. 2.11, 17, 26; 3.5, 12, 21; 21.7). In each of these references, the words clearly imply a fight of faith for the follower of Christ. Therefore, perseverance is not an act of God for a believer, but the action of the believer in response to the command of Christ to continue in His Word and grace.

In considering perseverance, two questions immediately present themselves: **1)** What is God's role? **2)** What is man's role? Phil. 2.13 says that God works in us, both to will and to do His good pleasure). But how is this work accomplished in us? It is by His grace. Paul shows that it is by grace that our walk with Him begins (Eph. 2.8-9), and in another place this same grace teaches us that *"denying ungodliness and worldly lusts, we should live soberly, righteously, and godly, in this present world,"* and to *"look for that blessed hope, and the glorious appearing of the great God and our Savior Jesus Christ"* (Titus 2.11-13). Further, God's grace is able to keep us faultless with joy (Jude 24). It is important to understand, however, that man must respond in faith and accept the grace He has provided for him (Rom. 10.9-10). It is at the crisis moment of transforming faith that man begins his walk with God; but just as man turns to God for saving grace, he must also seek Him for sustaining grace (Mt. 7.7-11, 21-27; Lk. 8.15; 11.28; Jn. 14.15, 23; Jude 24). Man's perseverance depends on his continued desire to walk with the Lord (Jn. 8.31; Col. 1.23; Jude 21). This is shown further by the original New Testament word, *sozo*, that signifies "to save." This word is expressed in three tenses: "I am saved," "I am being saved,"

"I shall be saved." Thus, man must be willing to continue to *"press"* into the kingdom of God, and to persevere at all costs in order to be finally saved (Lk. 9.23; 16.16).

The commandment to *persevere—endure, abide*—in Christ carries eternal consequences. The inheritance of eternal life hinges on the Christian's decision to continue to seek the grace of God and to walk in obedience to His Word. We must be *"willing and obedient"* (Is. 1.19) and *"willing to live honestly"* (Heb. 13.18). According to the apostle John, if an individual does not remain in the doctrine of Christ, he does not have God, and he that does not have the Son of God does not have life (2 Jn. 9; 1 Jn. 5.12); therefore, the judgment for those who do not persevere is eternal damnation and separation from God (Mt. 25.41-46, Heb. 10.26-27).

Practical Graces

Restitution is the act of restoring something wrongfully taken, or the satisfying of one whom otherwise has been wronged (Mt. 3.8; Lk. 19.8-9). This act alone does not save, but it gives evidence of a heart that has truly repented. Restitution glorifies the grace of God and supports the testimony of the believer. It also gives opportunity to reconcile with those who have been wronged. It is the fulfillment of the law of love (Rom. 13.8). Some restitutions should be made only with great care and with pastoral guidance, in order to avoid further offense or injury.

Sabbath means rest. Observance of the Sabbath in the Old Testament (the seventh day) was instituted to point to the believer's spiritual rest in Christ under the New Covenant. The Old Testament requirement to keep the Sabbath holy is now superseded by the commandment: *"Be ye holy,"* for in Christ the believer is enabled and required to live holy every day. Sunday is not the Sabbath, but is a day set aside by the church to give special attention to the worship of God and the fellowship of the saints (Hos. 2.11; Col. 2.16-17; Rom. 14.5-6; Heb. 4.1-11).

Meats and Drinks—The prohibitions against certain meats and drinks in the Old Testament were not extended into the New Testament church. These ceremonial aspects of Mosaic legislation were *"nailed* *to the cross"* of Christ and done away with in the covenant of grace (Col. 2.13-17; Eph. 2.15; Heb. 9.8-11). What one eats and drinks (with the exception of intoxicating beverages) is now a matter of conscience, and does not violate the nature and principles of the kingdom of God (Rom. 14.17). However, one should be mindful of the Scriptural injunction: *". . . whatsoever ye do, do all to the glory of God"* (1 Cor. 10.31; see also: Rom. 14.2; 1 Cor. 8.8; 1 Tim. 4.1-5).

Tithing and Giving—Tithing is the giving of one tenth of one's increase to Christ, our High Priest. It began as a voluntary act with Abraham, was required under the Mosaic law, and carried forward by Christ as a discipline for the New Testament church (Mt. 23.23). Tithes are to be brought to the house of God and properly distributed by the ministers having charge of the treasury (Mal. 3.10). Freewill offerings are to be encouraged and regarded as a gift from the heart. Tithing and giving into the church are part of God's plan to finance His work through the church on earth. We are required in the Scriptures to be good stewards of that which God has entrusted in our care (See also: Gen. 14.18-20; Lk. 11.42; 1 Cor. 16.2; 2 Cor. 9.6-9; Heb. 7.1-21).

Swearing and Profanity—Taking an oath is contrary to the spirit of the New Testament. *"But above all things, my brethren, swear not, neither by heaven, neither by the earth, neither by any other oath: but let your yea be yea; and your nay, nay; lest ye fall into condemnation"* (Jas. 5.12). Jesus said, *"But I say unto you, Swear not at all...But let your communication be, Yea, yea; Nay, nay: for whatsoever is more than these cometh of evil"* (Mt. 5.34, 37; see also Ex. 20.7). An affirmation of the truth is sufficient; it is acceptable even in secular courts. Similarly, the use of profanity reflects an impure heart and has no place in the life of a child of God (Mt. 15.18-19; Phil. 1.27; 3.20; 1 Pet. 1.15; 2 Pet. 2.7; Jas. 3.8-10).

Intoxicating Beverages and Drugs— *"Wine is a mocker, strong drink is raging: and whosoever is deceived thereby is not wise"* (Prov. 20.1). The Scriptures teach against the consumption of alcohol or other intoxicating beverages because God has called us to perfect sobriety (1 Pet. 5.8; 1 Thess. 5.6; Tim. 3.2; Titus 2.2). Believers are admonished not to *" . . . give place to the devil."* So-called moderate or social drinking certainly gives place to the adversary, and thus believers should totally abstain (Eph. 4. 27; see also: Is. 28.7; 1 Cor. 5.11; 6.10; Gal. 5.21). Much of what is said about intoxicating beverages is true also of drugs. The use of drugs such as tobacco, marijuana, opium, cocaine, etc., impair the body and is not in keeping with the teachings and principles of Christ and the Scriptures. These things defile the body and are inconsistent with God's call to soberness (2 Cor. 7.1; Is. 55.2; 1 Cor. 10.31-32; Eph. 5.3-8; Jas. 1.21). Drugs used for medical purposes should be taken only under the care and direction of a physician, and then only in good conscience.

Gambling ("Gaming")—Zion Assembly is opposed to gambling in any form. Gambling brings with it a negative effect on society and is immoral (Ex. 20.17; 1 Tim. 6.9-10). This sin is associated with wasting time, money, and possessions. It also carries with it the stigma of greed and covetousness (see Ex. 20.17; Ps. 10.3; I Cor. 6.9-10; Eph. 5.5; 1 Tim. 6.9-10; Heb. 13.5). Gambling of any kind (lotteries, casinos, sports betting, video poker, (slot) machines, on-line gambling, bingo, etc.) is denounced in principle throughout Scripture. It is also addictive, leads to increased crime, and often destroys marriages and homes.

Unequal Yoke—The Bible teaches against the children of God being unequally yoked with unbelievers. Binding ourselves with unbelievers in organizations and secret orders with an oath is contrary to the Spirit of Christ and the plain teaching in the Scriptures (1 Cor. 6.14-17). As the espoused bride of Christ, we have covenanted ourselves to give undivided loyalty to Christ. *"For I am jealous over you with godly jealousy: for I have espoused you to one husband, that I may present you as a chaste virgin to Christ"* (2 Cor. 11.2; Jer. 50.5). Membership in organizations which require an oath of secrecy should be dissolved before becoming a member of the church. *"Jesus answered him, I spake openly to the world; I ever taught in the synagogue, and in the temple, whither the Jews always resort; and in secret have I said nothing"* (Jn. 18.20).

168

Spirit Baptism and Spiritual Gifts

Baptism with the Holy Ghost is an instantaneous experience wrought in the life of the believer subsequent to entire sanctification. In this baptism, Christ is the agent; the Spirit is the element (Mt. 3.11). The baptism with the Spirit on the sanctified life is accompanied with speaking in tongues: *"And they were all filled with the Holy Ghost, and began to speak with other tongues, as the Spirit gave them utterance"* (Acts 2.2-4; see also: 10.44-47; 19.1-6). The baptism with the Spirit is a baptism of spiritual empowerment for service in the kingdom of God (Lk. 24.49; Jn. 15.26; Acts 1.8); it also enables one to minister effectively within the church for the self-edification of the body (1 Cor. 12.12-28; Eph. 4.11-16).

Speaking in Tongues always accompanies the baptism with the Holy Ghost. The believer speaks in *"unknown tongues"* as *"the Spirit gives utterance"* (Acts 2.4). *"Unknown tongues"* is distinguished from *"divers tongues,"* that is, in languages that are known to man (Acts 2.6; 1 Cor. 12.10; 14.2). In either case, *"unknown tongues"* or languages known to man, and the manifestation of tongues and interpretations must always be consistent with the Word of God (1 Cor. 14.26). The gift of tongues is a sign to unbelievers (vv. 14.21-23), but serves also for the self-edification of the believer (v. 4).

Gifts Of The Spirit—There are various gifts and operations of the Holy Ghost (1 Cor. 12.4-11). The gifts of the Spirit were in operation in the New Testament church, but thereafter the church began to *"fall away"* and the manifestations of the spiritual gifts began to wane. After the apostasy in the fourth century, and the ensuing *"dark ages"* of Christian history, the manifestations of spiritual gifts (particularly tongues-speaking) were almost non-existent (manifested on occasion mainly among so-called heretics and unorthodox Christians). In these last days (particularly since early in the twentieth century) God is again pouring out His Spirit *"upon all flesh"* according to prophecy in order to fulfill His eternal purpose through the church (Joel 2.28-32; 3.16-18; Acts 2.38-39).

Signs Following Believers—Signs in the New Testament were mainly for the purpose of confirming the Word of God and Jesus Christ as the promised Messiah. As believers went forth preaching the Word in Jesus' name, the Lord worked with them and confirmed the Word with signs following (Mk. 16.15-20). Miraculous signs follow believers in order to confirm the proclamation of the Word of God, to convict sinners, and to edify the body of Christ (Mk. 16.17; 1 Cor. 12.12-31).

Ordinances

Water Baptism is the act of being immersed in water by the minister of the Gospel in the name of the Father, Son and Holy Ghost. It is commanded by Christ and represents His death, burial and resurrection, which are experienced in the life of the believer (Rom. 6.3-5). This ordinance has no power to wash away sin, but is the answer of a good conscience toward God (1 Pet. 3.21). Water baptism is valid only when the candidate is actually born again (Mt. 28.19; Mk. 1.8-10; 16.15-16; Jn. 3.:22-23; Acts 10.47- 48; 16.3). Water baptism is identified with spiritual regeneration; it is not the door into the church.

Lord's Supper is a memorial meal, which calls to remembrance the sacrifice of Christ, who shed His blood for our sins. Jesus commanded that this sacred meal be observed *"in remembrance of me"* (1 Cor. 11.24). The broken, unleavened bread represents His body; the fruit of the vine (unfermented grape juice) represents His blood. This sacred ordinance should be observed with holy reverence, only after careful self-examination (1 Cor. 10. 16-17; 11.23-30). It is the outward sign of Christ's covenant with the church (Lk. 22.20).

Feet Washing is an ordinance in the church. Following the institution of the Lord's Supper, Christ girded himself with a towel, washed the disciples' feet, and said: *"If I, then, your Lord and Master, have washed your feet; ye also ought to wash one another's feet"* (Jn. 13.14). This ordinance is distinguished from the cultural practice of feet washing in the Middle East; it has spiritual significance and is commanded to be observed by believers (1 Tim. 5.10). The purpose of feet washing is not fulfilled through charity and good works. It is to remind us that we have one Master and Lord, who is the head of the church, and we are all His servants, and servants of one another.

Proclamation and Public Reading of the Word of God—

The Bible, the written Word of God, is a visible sign and witness pointing men to the Gospel of Christ. The Bible is a sacred record or witness of Jesus' birth, death, resurrection, ascension, glorification, and on-going intercessory work in unity with the Father in His heavenly throne (Acts 7.55; Rev. 3.21). It is a written revelation of the saving work of God in Christ, and thus analogous to God's Word inbreathed into the hearts of believers.

God's church is bound by a sacred covenant to read, study, and obey the Word of God. Each member is to read, hear, believe, receive, search, study, and obey the Word of God. The church is to proclaim *"all the counsel of God"* (Acts 20.27), teach believers in all nations *"to observe all things whatsoever that [Christ has commanded]"* (Mt. 28.19-20, and to *"rightly divide the word of truth."* (2 Tim. 2.15).

The public reading of the Word of God is pure proclamation, allowing the Word to speak for itself. The Reading of Holy Scriptures is commanded and encouraged in both Old and New Testaments, and otherwise taught by precept and example by Christ, the apostles, and prophets.

The practice of the proclamation and public reading of the Bible demonstrates a sober reverence for the written Word of God. In an age in which the majority of professing Christians are biblically illiterate and falling away from confidence in the Bible as God's infallible Word written in Scripture, and consequently from serious Bible reading the study, God's church stands out like a *"city set on a hill"* holding forth the light of His Word!

The proclamation and public reading of the Word of God serves to reveal the mind of God; aids in personal and corporate cleansing of the believer; edifies the believer; comforts the believer; and encourages and strengthens corporate unity among believers. Where observed with sobriety, sincerity, and gravity the "Proclamation and Public Reading of Scripture" can produce revival, restoration, and reconciliation (Ex. 24.7-8; Josh. 8.34-35; 2 Kgs. 23.1-20; Neh. 8.1-8, 14-18; 2 Cor. 5.18-20). As such, proclamation, public reading, and responsive readings of the Sacred Scriptures bear all the marks of an ordinance, and thus should be observed as a divine order of worship, ministry, and theocratic administration.

Ministry / Ordination—The church recognizes the ordination and function of the ministry as an ordinance of God placed in the church to reveal Christ and demonstrate spiritual truth. Much like "Water Baptism," the act of *"laying on of hands"* for ordination is the church acting instrumentally to physically demonstrate God's spiritual calling and appointment of an individual as a servant leader in God's church. By acting instrumentally under the guidance of the Holy Spirit to ordain ministers, the church also reveals and demonstrates true theocracy.

Not only does the act of ordination demonstrate a spiritual truth, but the function of ministry has been ordained by God to serve as a revelation of Christ and His ministry to the world. Christ is the "Great Shepherd" (pastor) who lovingly oversees His flock (1 Pet. 5.1-4). He is the ultimate servant minister who came to *"serve"* (minister) and to be *"served"* (ministered to) (Mt. 20.28; Philem. 2.5-8). Christ has established and ordained the ministry to mirror and reveal His ministry. As the minister serves the flock, tends the flock, watches over the flock, and gives his life for the flock, the minister visibly demonstrates the heart and work of Christ. The membership practices this ordination and aids in this revelation by honoring the ministry and willingly submitting to those who have the rule over them (Heb. 13.7, 17) thus demonstrating the Christian's honor of God and submission to God's government (Col. 3.23-24; Eph. 5.22).

The Church is a divine institution and **bears all the marks** of an ordinance. It has been ordained by God to be the *"light of the world, a city set upon an hill"* (Mt. 5.14). As such it is designed to be the sacred embodiment of truth symbolizing and declaring the mysteries of God to the world through the power of the Holy Ghost. It is the *"Body of Christ and members in particular"* (1 Cor. 12.27) all working together to be the physical representation of Christ in the world. It is the *"house of God,"* (1 Tim. 3.15) the *"temple of God"* (Eph. 2.21; 1 Cor. 3.16) consisting of *"living stones"* (1 Pet. 2.5) *"fitly framed together and builded together for an habitation of God through the Spirit"* (Eph. 2.21-22). By *"binding and loosing on earth what has been bound and* *loosed in Heaven"* (Mt. 16.19), the church serves as a revelation of both the invisible God and His invisible Kingdom. The church preaches the Gospel, teaches the doctrine, lives the truth, practices government, submission, and discipline. The church embodies the Gospel for it consists of members who act as witnesses of the transforming power of Christ and His Gospel. *"But ye are a chosen generations, a royal priesthood, an holy nation, a peculiar people; that ye should shew forth the praises of him who hath called you out of darkness into his marvellous light..."* (1 Pet. 2.9). As such, the church serves as an ordinance. In fact, it is the ordinance which embodies and practices all the other ordinances.

Marriage is defined by God as a covenant between an eligible male and eligible female to become husband and wife and it is for life; as such it is a divine institution that should be held in the highest esteem among all men and women. The ordinance of marriage was instituted by God, reaffirmed by Christ, and given further emphasis and clarity by the apostles, and accordingly, practiced by the New Testament churches.

The first marriage ceremony was administered by God after the creation of man. Thus, marriage is the Genesis ordinance, the original ordinance. Marriage is an ordinance in that it acts as a universal witness of God's divine order for the human race (Mal. 2.14-16; Mt. 19.4-5; 1 Cor. 7.2-5, 14; Heb. 13.4; Eph. 5.22-32; Rev. 19.7-8). It is also a channel through which the human race, and more particularly the church of God, is divinely ordered and sustained in holiness and truth. (Mk. 10.6-9; 1 Cor. 7.14-16; Eph. 5.22-32). Perhaps most importantly, the ordinance of marriage is a symbol of salvation and the sacred union between God and His people as bridegroom and bride (Ex. 19.5; Song 5.1; 6.2-9; Is. 49.14-18; 62.5; Ezek. 16.8; Jn. 3.29; Mt. 22.2; 2 Cor. 11.2-3; Eph. 5.25-32; Rev. 19.7-8). Thus, God repeatedly uses marriage terms to explain His relationship with the church, a relationship which culminates in the Bridegroom coming to take His bride to the Father's house for the marriage supper (Rev. 19.7; Eph. 5.25-27; Jn. 14.1-3; Mt. 25.1-10).

The members of the church aid in and practice this ordinance by reflecting Christ and the church through their marriage relationships. The husband loves the wife and gives himself for her (Eph. 5.25-29) while the wife loves her husband and submits to his loving authority (Eph. 5.22-24).

Divine Sanctities

Sanctity of Life—Human life is sacred because it is created in the image of God (Gen. 1.27). Taking of innocent life is thus strictly forbidden in Scripture, including abortion, infanticide, euthanasia, genocide, and suicide (self-murder). *"Thou shalt not kill"* (Ex. 20.13). Whosoever sheddeth innocent blood will not be held guiltless before God (Gen. 9.6; Num. 35.30-31; Rom. 13.8-10; Rev. 21.8).

Sanctity of Marriage—Jesus said, "Have ye not read, that he which made them at the beginning made them male and female. For this cause shall a man leave his father and mother, and shall cleave to his wife: and they twain shall be one flesh: Wherefore they are no more twain, but one flesh. What therefore God hath joined together, let not man put asunder" (Mt.19:4-6). Accordingly, marriage is a divine institution between a male and female until death (Mk. 10.2-12; Rom. 7:2; 1 Cor. 7.39) and as such it should be held in the highest esteem among all men and women.

Marriage is for life, and therefore divorce for any reason, including unfaithfulness, cannot dissolve a marriage. (The "exception" to this rule mentioned in Mt. 5.32 and 19.9 will be explained below). Thus remarriage after a divorce (while the first companion is still living) constitutes the sin of adultery (see Lk. 16.18; Ex. 20:14, 17; Mal. 2.14-17; 1 Cor. 5.1-5; 6: 15-20; 7.2, 3).

While the Bible commends marriage, and sex within marriage, it clearly condemns sex before or outside of marriage (Heb. 13.4). This condemnation includes sexual relations which might occur between a couple while "living together" or "cohabiting" in a non-married state (see 1 Cor. 5.1- 5; 6. 15-20; 7.2, 3).

Marriage is between one man and one woman for life; therefore sexual relations are lawful only within a God-ordained and biblically recognized marriage. Adultery (which includes remarriage while one's first companion is still living), polygamy, and fornication (which includes pre-marital sex and cohabitation) are therefore sinful practices that violate the law of God, and injure the home and family.

The meaning of the word fornication has been the subject of much debate. Fornication is sometimes used in Scripture in a broad sense to include all forms of sexual immorality. However, when fornication and adultery are used in the same text, fornication usually refers to unlawful sexual relations before a person has been joined in a biblical, covenant marriage. This is certainly the case in Mt. 5.32 and 19.9. In these references, fornication signified unlawful sexual relations during the ancient, Jewish betrothal period—that is, before the betrothed couple had consummated their marriage (confer Mt.1.18-25). Fornication in this context would include also, however, a single person who has married someone else's companion, that is, a divorced person. And it would apply also to an incestuous relationship—a sin of which the believers in Jesus' day were well aware (1 Cor. 5.1-9; Leviticus 18.6-20; see also Acts 15.29, for the reference here by the Jerusalem council seems to indicate this kind of fornication).

In any case, fornication includes a single person who has been joined to another unlawfully in marriage. This was the gross form of fornication in the Corinthian church that Paul so boldly reproved, and for which cause he demanded that the church withdraw fellowship from the violator—"To deliver such a one unto Satan for the destruction of the flesh, that the spirit may be saved in the day of the Lord Jesus" (1 Cor. 5.1-9). It was in this context also that the apostle commanded that in order to avoid the sin of fornication, *"let every man have his own wife, and let every woman have her own husband"* (1 Cor.7.2; see also Mk. 6.16-18; 1 Cor. 5.1). In Gal. 5.19, both adultery and fornication are listed as works of the flesh, and the apostle solemnly warns that *"they which do such things shall not inherit the kingdom of God."* For these reasons, those who are entangled in these sins and unlawful marriages are not eligible for membership in the Lord's church (confer 1 Jn. 3.7-10; 1 Cor. 5.11; 6.9-10).

Sanctity of the Body—Our body is the temple of the Holy Spirit, and we are admonished to glorify God in our body (1 Cor. 6.20-21). "If any man defile the temple of God, him shall God destroy" (3.16-17). We are also admonished to present our bodies "a living sacrifice, holy, acceptable unto God" (Rom. 12.1), and " . . . whatsoever ye do, do all to the glory of God" (1 Cor. 10.31b). Incest, same sex unions, and all homosexual and lesbian relationships are strictly forbidden by the Scriptures. These practices are an abomination to God, though they may be sanctioned by a state or religious institution (Rom. 1.24-28; Lev. 18.22-23; 20.10-21). Practices such as "body piercing," tattooing, mutilating and disfiguring the body are of pagan origin and contrary to the spirit of holiness and biblical principles. These practices should have no place in the lives of believers (cf: Tim. 2.8-10; Rom. 12.1-2; Is. 3.16-22; 1 Jn. 2.15-17).

Eschatology
Scenario of Endtime Events

Rapture and Pre-Millennial Second Coming Of Jesus—
Christ is coming again in the clouds of heaven with power and great glory (Mt. 24.27-28). *"The dead in Christ shall rise first, then we which are alive and remain shall be caught up together with them in the clouds to meet the Lord in the air and so shall we ever be with the Lord"* (1 Thess. 4.16-18; see also 1 Cor. 15.51-52). All who are caught up in the first resurrection will attend the marriage supper of the Lamb (Rev. 19.7-9). Christ will then return to earth and reign with the saints for a thousand years (vv. 4, 6; see also Zech. 14.4-5; 1 Thess. 4.14; Jude 14-15; Rev. 5.10; 19.11-21).

Resurrection—There will be a resurrection for both the righteous and the wicked. The righteous will be raised at Christ's first appearance in the clouds of glory. The resurrection of the wicked will occur after the thousand years reign of Christ on earth. *"And have hope toward God, which they themselves also allow, that there shall be a resurrection of the dead, both of the just and unjust"* (Acts 24.15; see also Dan. 12.2; Rev. 20.4-6; Jn. 5.28-29; 1 Cor. 15.12-23, 41-58).

Eternal Life for the Righteous—The reward of the righteous is everlasting life in the presence of God. *"And these shall go away into everlasting punishment: but the righteous into life eternal"* (Mt. 25.46; Lk. 18.29, 30; Jn. 10.28; Rom. 6.22; 1 Jn. 5.11-13)

Eternal Punishment for the Wicked—Those who reject or disregard the call to repentance and salvation are doomed to eternal damnation (Jn. 3.15-21). In hell there is no escape, no liberation, no annihilation. Hell is *"the second death,"* and is a place of eternal torment. *"But the fearful, and unbelieving, and the abominable, and murderers, and whoremongers, and sorcerers, and idolaters, and all*

liars, shall have their part in the lake which burneth with fire and brimstone: which is the second death" (Rev. 21.8; see also: 20.10-15; 2 Thess. 1.7-10; Jude 14, 15; Mt. 25.46; Mk. 3.29).

Antichrist—Antichrist can signify either "against Christ" or "in the place of Christ," or a combination of the two meanings. Antichrist is one who opposes Christ or who assumes the prerogatives of Christ as our Lord and Savior.

While only the apostle John uses the word, antichrist, the apostle Paul is apparently speaking of the same spirit and principle when he refers to the "mystery of lawlessness" and the "lawless one" in 2 Thess. 2.3, 8. John identifies certain *"false prophets"* and *"deceivers"* as antichrists (1 Jn. 4.1-3; 2.18; 2 Jn. 7). The prophet Daniel is in reference to this same spirit in his prophecy of the *"beast"* in Dan. 7, which corresponds with John's vision of the "beast" in Rev., chapters 11; 13; 17; 19.

We may conclude then that the spirit of antichrist signifies the deceptive and seductive spirit in the world that seeks to confuse the true identity of Christ and to corrupt His Gospel. Antichrist may take many religious, social, and political forms, but all have the same goal—namely, to compromise and corrupt the true doctrine of salvation in Jesus Christ with false doctrines and the pretense of false Christs (Mt. 24.4-5, 11, 23, 24).

Prophecy predicts that a particular person in the very last days will come on the scene that will embody and personify the spirit of antichrist in the world. This man is variously characterized as the *"lawless one"* (2 Thess. 2.3, 8) and the *"beast"* (Dan. 7.10-11, 25; Rev. 13.1). Jesus is in reference to this spirit of deception and lawlessness in Mt. 24.5, 24 and Jn. 5.43. Our concern in the church, however, is not so much with the coming of the particular Lawless One—*"the beast"*—but with the spirit of antichrist now prevailing in the world: for it seems that the prophetic Lawless One will not be fully revealed until after the rapture of the church (2 Thess. 2.7-8). Until then, the Spirit of God and the church will restrain and prevent his rise to power and his full revelation.

God's church rests upon the Revelation—the *"rock"*—that Jesus Christ is the Son of the living God (Mt. 16.13-18), and that He was incarnate in the virgin Mary, died for our sins, and was resurrected on the third day so that man can be redeemed and brought back into fellowship with God our Father (Rom. 5.6-10). The Spirit of Christ indwells believers, enabling them to live their lives consistent with the law of God (Rom. 8.1-7); whereas the spirit of antichrist opposes the truth of God revealed in the Holy Scriptures, providing substitutions for the saving grace of Christ. The diabolic influence of antichrist is found throughout the world, resisting the true Gospel and substituting in its place myriads of false gospels (Gal. 1.1-9; 2 Cor. 11.3-4). These are *"lying spirits"* set to deceive and destroy precious souls (2 Thess. 2.9; Rev. 13.13-14). John exhorts believers to *"try the spirits"*—test them, prove them—against the truth of Christ and His teachings revealed in the Scriptures (1 Jn. 4.1-3). The spirit of antichrist, personified in the Lawless One, will be completely destroyed with the brightness of Christ's second coming and the power of His Word (2 Thess. 2.8). Meanwhile the saints are empowered to resist and overcome the spirit of antichrist in the world through faith, the Word of God, and the power of the Holy Spirit.

Principles for Practical Christian Living and Discipline

The following guidelines are explicitly revealed in the Scriptures or else shown to be consistent with biblical teachings. They are brought to our attention to enhance our relationship with Christ and one another, and to encourage us to live in a way that will bring glory and honor to the name of Christ and to support the witness of the church. We are admonished in the Scriptures: *" . . . be thou an example of the believers, in word, in conversation, in charity, in spirit, in faith, in purity"* (1 Tim. 4.12). Jesus instructs us: *"Let your light so shine before men, that they may see your good works, and glorify your Father which is in heaven"* (Mt. 5.16).

Prayer—Jesus' admonition to *"watch and pray"* (Mt. 26.41) has never been more urgent than today. We live in *"perilous times,"* and Christ and the apostles warned that the times will only worsen as we approach our Lord's return. Therefore, daily prayers and family devotions should be a priority in every church home. Maintaining a prayerful attitude is a key to spirituality for every individual and local congregation. Again Jesus said, *"...men ought always to pray, and not to faint"* (Lk. 18.1), and the apostle encouraged believers to *"pray without ceasing "* (1 Thess. 5.17). We are also enjoined to *" . . . pray one for another . . .* Jas. 5.16a).

Special prayers should be made for those in authority and for those who have given themselves in service to God and to the ministry of the Word (1 Tim. 2.1-3). Prayer is so essential to the life of the church that the church is called *"the house of prayer"* (Is. 56.7; Mt. 21.13).

Bible Study—Reading and studying the Scriptures are invaluable to the spiritual welfare of the child of God. Every member of the church is encouraged to be a faithful student of God's holy Word. Paul instructs us to *"Study to shew thyself approved unto God . . . "* (2 Tim 2.15a), for *"the holy scriptures are able to make thee wise unto salvation through faith which is in Christ Jesus"* (3.15). Further, he says, *"All scripture is given by inspiration of God, and is profitable for doctrine, for reproof, for correction, for instruction in righteousness"* (v.16). The importance of the Word of God is eloquently expressed by Psalmist: *"Thy word is a lamp unto my feet, and a light unto my path."* And again, *"Thy word have I hid in mine heart, that I might not sin against thee"* (Psalm 119.105, 11).

Church Attendance and Worship—Worship and fellowship with believers of *"like precious faith"* is a vital part of the Christian life. Worship should be heartfelt in the Spirit, and in harmony with the Word of God (Jn. 4.23; Eph. 5.19). Each member of the church is a part of the body of Christ, and thus the body will be hindered to the degree that one member fails to actively participate in its life and mission. Accordingly, members should actively support every function of the church, and participate as much as possible. The exhortation of the Hebrew writer is worthy of our careful attention: *"And let us consider one another to provoke unto love and good works. "Not forsaking the assembling of ourselves together, as the manner of some; but exhorting one another: and so much more as we see the day approaching"* (Heb. 10.25). Children should be instructed at home, and taught by precept and example to respect the house of God. Ministers and their families should be examples in their lifestyles and conversations. *"And they shall teach my people the difference between the holy and profane"* (Ezek. 44.23). A prayerful attitude creates an atmosphere conductive for worship and the ministry of God's Word. Believers should therefore be prayerful as the minister delivers the message, lest Satan come and steal the Word of God from their hearts (Mk. 4.4, 15). God's love *"shed abroad in our hearts by the Holy Ghost"* should fill the atmosphere

179

of our worship services. Love should govern our every action and be shown to everyone without partiality (1 Cor. 13). We should take special care to show love to visitors. Jesus said, *"By this shall all men know that ye are my disciples, if ye have love one to another"* (Jn. 13.35).

Walking Circumspectly—Children of God should *"walk circumspectly, not as fools, but as wise, Redeeming the time for the days are evil"* (Eph. 5.15-16). Living a consecrated life at home and abroad will give no place for anyone to justly think or speak of you as a hypocrite. Our manner of life and conversation should be holy in word and deed, as becoming to a child of God. As representatives of Christ in this world, and members of the Church of God, we should fashion ourselves with modesty and sobriety (Ps. 1.1-3; Phil. 1.27; 1 Thess. 5.15-23).

Entertainment and Worldly Attractions—Christians should never participate in worldly attractions and entertainment where the principles of holiness may be compromised. Believers should participate in activities with unbelievers only with a guarded disposition, lest one becomes entangled or entrapped in the snares of Satan. *"Be sober, be vigilant; because your adversary the devil, as a roaring lion, walketh about, seeking whom he may devour"* (1 Pet. 5.8; see also 2 Pet. 2.19-22).

Illicit Relationships—Paul admonishes us to *"give no place to the devil"* (Eph. 4.27). Forming too close an intimacy with the opposite sex, even if they are brothers and sisters in the Lord, creates an environment for temptation and gives opportunity for the *"wiles of the devil."* Samson is a classic case of this unwise behavior, which led to his fall from grace (Judg. 16); whereas Joseph wisely fled from a similar situation (Gen. 39). Paul perhaps had Joseph in mind when he exhorted, *"Flee fornication"* (1 Cor. 6.18). The words of James, the Lord's brother, also come to mind: *"Lust when it is conceived bringeth forth sin, and sin when it is finished bringeth forth death"* (Jas. 1.13-15). In view of these solemn admonitions, great care should be taken to avoid associations and situations, which could reflect upon one's character and bring reproach upon Christ and the church.

Outward Adornment—Christians are both the servants and ambassadors of Jesus Christ. As His servants, our focus should always be to walk pleasing in His sight. God told Samuel *". . . for the LORD seeth not as man seeth; for man looketh on the outward appearance, but the LORD looketh on the heart"* (1 Sam. 16.7). As such, our primary focus should not be on adorning our outward person, but the "hidden man of the heart." We are informed that the character traits of the inner man—"modesty," "shamefacedness," "sobriety," and the "ornament of a meek and quiet spirit," etc., (1 Tim.2.9-10; 1 Pet. 3.3-4) are *"in the sight of God of great price."*

At the same time, however, our outward appearance is viewed also by men and therefore the saints of God should reflect a Christ-like character and witness (2 Cor. 3.2-3; 5.20; 8.21). As ambassadors for Christ, we should dress in a manner which represents Christ and His values to the world. Those *"professing godliness"* should be holy in their appearance and should never adorn themselves in provocative, seductive, and gaudy clothing and/or cosmetics [lipsticks, eye shadows, etc.] which create a superficial beauty, and which tend to contradict and confuse the godly qualities of "lowliness," "wholesomeness," "holiness," "sobriety," "meekness," "gravity," "purity," and Christ-likeness. For the Lord "[beautifies] the meek with salvation" (Ps. 149.4).

To be sure, our primary and most important emphasis should be on manifesting the inner graces of the Spirit which result from the new birth—love, patience, faith, hope, godly contentment, peace, gentleness, meekness, mercy, sobriety, gravity, etc.; but we are admonished also to adorn the doctrine of God (Titus 2.10), which includes the outward signs of salvation—"lifting holy hands," "praying," "praise," "rejoicing" ["shouting," "clapping of the hands," etc.], "thankfulness," "good works," and a "meek and quiet spirit." Further, it must include also dressing in modest apparel, which logically precludes the wearing of jewelry, gold, pearls, and costly array (1Tim. 2.9-10; Titus 2.3, 10; 1 Pet. 3.3-5).

It is true that there are many references in the Old Testament that show that God's people under the Old Covenant adorned themselves with jewels and precious stones. But as we move from the Old Testament to the New, we find that these ornaments of gold and silver and precious jewels were symbolic of the inward graces of salvation. Thus, the prophet Isaiah wrote, *"I will greatly rejoice in the Lord, my soul shall be joyful in my God; for He has clothed me with the garments of salvation, He has covered me with the robe of righteousness, as a bridegroom decks himself with ornaments, and as a bride adorns herself with her jewels"* (Is. 61.10). In point of fact, the members of the church are themselves the "jewels" of God (Mal. 3.17). We should seek therefore to cultivate the inner light of the Holy Spirit in our lives, in order to be a *"city set on a hill"* to manifest the light and glory of God's holiness before a watching world.

Both the inner graces of the indwelling Spirit and our modest outward dress and behavior give witness to the attributes and fruit of believers who have been transformed by the grace and power of Christ, and who have been informed in regard to His teachings and have fully committed themselves to reflect His holy image.

Corporate and Self-Discipline—Self-examinations to evaluate one's own faith and spirituality are healthy (1 Cor. 11:28). Sincere concern for others is also good and to be encouraged. We are our brother's keeper. Counsel should be given only in the spirit of love and with godly wisdom, and according to the rule of discipline outlined in the gospel (Mt. 18.15-20). (A harsh spirit of criticism is detrimental to the spiritual welfare of both the critic and the one receiving the criticism: Mt. 7.1-5; 2 Cor. 2.1-11; Gal. 5.14-15; Eph. 4.30-32). Discipline should be administered only as a last resort, and always through prayerful counsel and with the ultimate good of the erring brother/sister in mind (1 Cor. 5.1-7; Gal. 6.1-5).

These 18th Annual Assembly Minutes were approved and verified by

Wade H. Phillips
Wade H. Phillips,
Presiding Bishop/Moderator

Wanda Busbee
Wanda Busbee, Chief Clerk

Made in the USA
Columbia, SC
22 August 2022

65200605R00104